ENTREPRENEURIAL REFLECTIONS

ONE ENTREPRENEUR'S

PERSONAL MOMENTS

THAT WILL EXPAND AND

CHANGE YOUR THINKING.

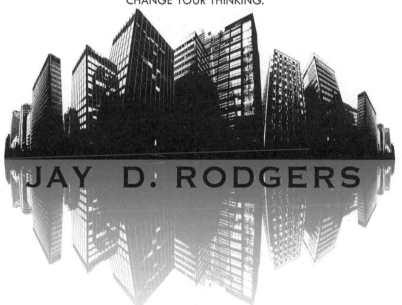

JAY D. RODGERS

Entrepreneurial Reflections:
One Entrepreneur's Personal Moments That
Will Expand and Change Your Thinking

© 2016 by Jay Rodgers

Published by Clovercroft Publishing, Franklin, Tennessee

Cover and Interior Layout Design by Debbie Manning Sheppard

Edited by Tammy Kling and Cari Schweichler

Printed in the United States of America

978-1-942557-95-1

ENTREPRENEURIAL
REFLECTIONS

ONE ENTREPRENEUR'S

PERSONAL MOMENTS

THAT WILL EXPAND AND

CHANGE YOUR THINKING.

JAY D. RODGERS

ENTREPRENEURIAL
REFLECTIONS

"ASK AND YE SHALL RECEIVE.

ENTREPRENEURS ALWAYS ASK."

JAY RODGERS

CONTENTS

ENTREPRENEURIAL
REFLECTIONS

"WHEN YOU'RE IN A NEGOTIATION,

CARE - BUT NOT TOO MUCH."

HERB COHEN

INTRODUCTION

TONY JEARY

ENTREPRENEURS ARE RISK TAKERS.

They take risks most corporate executives can't or won't because in the corporation, if you make a mistake, it could mean your job. Depending on the culture, mistakes can be costly. When you're an entrepreneur, a mistake impacts you the most, and you learn that mistakes are necessary on the path to growth.

Jay Rodgers has been my mentor along the journey to help me navigate countless deals and think differently in many ways. It's not just me that he's helped - his legacy has been to help entrepreneurs grow businesses that are successful, profitable, and sustainable. Jay grows businesses that create income and employment for many. Jay is the visionary for and co-founder of Biz Owners' Ed, an entrepreneurial think tank that was created because a small group of highly successful entrepreneurs believed in small business and the benefits it provides to America's economy and society.

Jay grew this group of dedicated entrepreneurs into a powerful mastermind willing to give back and help expand this country's seriously committed entrepreneurs by sharing advice from lessons they had learned. He is an extremely successful entrepreneur who has started, grown, and sold over a dozen companies that employ thousands of people and are worth hundreds of millions.

Because he appreciates the impact entrepreneurs can have on this great country, he has invested a great deal of his time over the years mentoring them one-on-one. He wanted to have a more powerful impact and a greater influence on more people than he could have with his own limited time, expertise, and contacts. So he stepped back and asked, "What can I devote the rest of my life to that would give ongoing perpetual motion to the fostering and support of successful entrepreneurship?" By leveraging his own database and connections, he co-founded Biz Owners' Ed. But, before he even became an entrepreneur he displayed entrepreneurial tendencies. As a kid, he made one of his first entrepreneurial decisions when he sold a saddle his parents had given him.

In the 1800s and well into the 1900s when cattle ranching still required a bunkhouse full of cowboys and a large remuda (herd of horses), cowboys often drifted from one cattle outfit to the next. They carried all of their earthly possessions with them. Since each cowboy needed several horses, the ranch furnished their mounts. It was, however, both a matter of practice and pride that the cowboys brought their most prized possession with them: their own personal saddle. To show up without your saddle was a disgrace. It indicated you had hit bottom and had been forced to sell your saddle. The expression that told the story was, "He sold his saddle."

In Jay's case, it wasn't selling his saddle but *trading* his saddle that put him in disgrace with his parents. Like most entrepreneurs, his first entrepreneurial venture didn't start out as one. Instead, it started with a nice gift from his parents of a youth saddle they had purchased for $50.00 from mass retailer and catalogue merchant Montgomery Ward's for his tenth birthday. While he was pleased with and grateful for the saddle, two years later at age 12, he was ready for a real man's saddle. Jay had his eye on a reconditioned stock saddle in a saddle shop he liked to visit. It wasn't new, but he wanted it. The sights and smells of a saddle shop are unique, and the saddle maker, Mr. Kennedy, was friendly with Jay and always had a great cowboy story ready. He had even repaired a saddle for Buffalo Bill Cody.

Jay somehow persuaded Mr. Kennedy to trade the stock saddle for the Montgomery Ward's saddle. But when he returned home with it, his parents were not happy because they felt his saddle was more valuable than the stock saddle. A few days later, Jay met a man that had also had his eye on the saddle he had acquired, so Jay promptly sold the stock saddle for $90. That was Jay's first big profit and entry into the world of entrepreneurial adventures! Going forward, Jay's parents' disappointment was replaced with support and encouragement for Jay's entrepreneurial ventures.

NO MATTER WHERE YOU STARTED, THERE'S ALWAYS A STORY ABOUT THE SPIRIT AND ADVENTURE OF BEING AN ENTREPRENEUR.

I've been an entrepreneur for years, from mowing lawns to now being a CEO strategist and coach as well as speaker who travels the world giving advice to leaders of companies of all sorts. Jay and I co-authored a powerful book together called *Advice Matters,* to teach people that you simply cannot do it alone. Advice does matter, and so does action, as Jay says. Whether you're an entrepreneur or an executive, the advice within the following pages will take you to new levels.

Jay and I working on our book, *Advice Matters*

Turn the page, and enjoy,

TONY JEARY

ENTREPRENEURIAL
REFLECTIONS

ONE ENTREPRENEUR'S

PERSONAL MOMENTS

THAT WILL EXPAND AND

CHANGE YOUR THINKING.

JAY D. RODGERS

ENTREPRENEURIAL
REFLECTIONS

"AS YOU TRAVEL THE

ENTREPRENEURIAL ROAD TO SUCCESS,

REMEMBER THERE ARE TWO MILES OF DITCH

FOR EACH MILE OF ROAD."

1

ENTREPRENEURS
TAKE RISKS

Entrepreneurs are a lot like cowboys. If you're not a risk taker, gunslinger, or willing to dodge a few bullets or bulls, you may not be well suited to be an entrepreneur. Most successful entrepreneurs I know take calculated risks and think they're going to win. No one wants to take a risk where you think you'll lose. But occasionally you do experience a loss, or maybe you make a bad decision, and that's okay. It's all part of the journey.

Before I set out on the journey to become an entrepreneur (formally), I worked for Kodak. I say "formally" because I was an entrepreneur from an early age, starting one business or another and always finding ways to make money. Many entrepreneurs who come to the table for advice started out that way. If you asked, they'd tell you they've always been inquisitive as a child and ready to create a business, even if it was a roadside lemonade stand. Entrepreneurs share a few common traits, and you'll find me talking about them in this book.

- ❖ **ONE: Entrepreneurs always ask**. They ask for the business, and sometimes they even ask for more than the other person wants to give.

- ❖ **TWO: Entrepreneurs always learn.** They tend to see every victory and even failures as a growth experience.

- ❖ **THREE: Entrepreneurs seize opportunity when they see it.** Make sure you're not at the movies when your ship comes in.

Four months after I transferred from Rochester, NY to Dallas with Kodak, a man in a rumpled white dress shirt came in the back door of the advertising department, walked into my office and said, "I'm with Elko stores, and my name is Pat." He told me he needed some window displays for several of their Dallas stores. At that time, we had beautiful 30x40 color photograph enlargements that we gave stores to use in their displays. I took him to our storage area, and we picked out the photographs he wanted. I asked him how he got to the office. He had flown into nearby Love Field and took a cab over. I offered to drive him to his downtown Dallas hotel thinking that Elko's display man would appreciate saving a little money on his expense account.

We hit it off immediately and on our way to the Adolphus Hotel where he was staying, I suggested that we go to lunch. He said that would be great, but he wanted to go by the hotel first to change shirts since he was rumpled from the flight. When we got there and went straight to the President's Suite, I knew I had missed something. Turns out he was *the* owner of the Elko card and photo stores located throughout the Midwest and was one of our division's largest customers. We went on to lunch, and we both really enjoyed getting acquainted. I told him about the 1,000 line Christmas ad that Kodak was going to run in the *Dallas Morning News* and suggested that he take out a tie-in ad next to ours on the page. He didn't respond. I took him back to his hotel and went back to work.

The next day, I called the *Dallas Morning News* and asked them to do a mockup of the ad with an Elko tie-in ad that covered the remainder of the page. My partner at Kodak and the ad department at the *Dallas Morning News* were sure that Elko wouldn't agree to the tie-in because they had never done so in the past. However, they played along with me as the new guy and agreed to do the mockup. Four or five days later, they gave me a nice mockup in a presentation folder. The next day, my phone rang and a man's voice asked, "How many offers have you had today for a free lunch?"

"Who is this?"

The man replied, "Why does it matter if it's free?" It was Pat. After lunch, we went back to Pat's suite and had a few drinks. I showed him the mockup of the ad from the *Dallas Morning News*, and he didn't say "yes," "no," or "go fish." I tossed the ad across the room and it fell behind the couch. After a few more drinks, we decided to go out again, and Pat suggested we go to an early dinner. I agreed, and he directed me to the Dallas Love Field Airport. There was a great restaurant on the 2nd floor of the airport, and I assumed that's where we were headed. Instead, when we went inside, Pat walked up to the Delta ticket desk and asked for two tickets to Vegas. I made the instant decision to go, but I didn't want my customer to pay for my ticket, so I threw my credit card on the counter to pay for mine.

We flew to Vegas, had dinner, and hit the tables. About 1:00 a.m., while at the craps table, Pat looked over and said, "I liked the tie-in ad. We will do it just like the mock-up."

Around 2 or 3 a.m., we got back on the plane. Our flight out had done a turnaround in L.A., and the same crew was taking it back to Dallas. One of the flight attendants stopped us, "Didn't you fellows just get off of this plane?"

Pat told her, "Yeah, we didn't like it."

We got back to the Adolphus Hotel shortly before 7 a.m., and I was, of course, wearing the same clothes from the day before. Pat told me the hotel gift shop sold dress shirts and ties. I dropped him off, bought a shirt and tie and stopped at a service station to change on my way to work. I went straight to see my boss, David Lamb, and told him the whole story, not sparing him any details. David was thrilled that I had a natural rapport with Pat, a man who had avoided Kodak management for years. He was, however, a bit concerned about my methods, especially since Vegas was not in our division's 10 state territory. "Jay," he said, "were you drunk when you decided to go to Vegas with Pat?"

"No. We enjoyed a few drinks, but I wasn't drunk."

"Did you put the flight on your Kodak Air Travel credit card?"

"No! See, I told you I wasn't drunk."

I seized the opportunity to jump on a plane with a client, even though it defied most corporate people's idea of logic and was a risky decision. It was a spur-of-the-moment opportunity that required a quick decision. Most corporate junior executives wouldn't have made that same decision. But, a lot of entrepreneurs might. Entrepreneurs are just different. They have to be able to take measured and calculated risks. A Welshman friend summed it up well when he said, "Jay, cut a walking stick when you find it."

Today I mentor entrepreneurs to become all they can be. I have a glass conference room table that has etchings of major deals I've participated in sandblasted right into the table. It's a great reminder, as we sit around this table and talk, of the various lessons I've learned along the way. The logo of one company that I invested in and suffered a big loss is embedded in an ugly dark cloud to remind me of a mistake I won't make again.

Entrepreneurs come to the table for many reasons. Some are in trouble, some need a sounding board, and others need to have the available options pointed out to them. More often than not, they're starting a new venture and need guidance. Who shows up? The ones who ask. Entrepreneurs ask. I mentor them, and when I truly realized how big the need was, I started an organization called Biz Owners' Ed (Bizownersed.org) to help support entrepreneurs. At Biz Owners' Ed, each entrepreneur has the opportunity to share and can discuss business challenges with expert mentors. It's a great forum where entrepreneurs get together for four hours once a week for ten consecutive weeks, experience presentations from extremely successful entrepreneurs and guest speakers, and receive personal mentoring. I think every city should have a chapter or an organization like it to help support entrepreneurs and help them discover the answers they need.

I love learning from others, another trait of entrepreneurs. The very best book for all entrepreneurs, a must for those starting a business, is one written by Norm Brodsky and Bo Burlingham entitled *Street Smarts*. In the book Norm writes:

> "Indeed, I believe it's such mental habits (habits that he describes in his book) that allow people to become successful entrepreneurs. I believe most people can develop the habits of mind I'm talking about and use them to acquire the wherewithal to live whatever kind of life they want. Not that every person will be successful to the same degree or in the same way. In business, as elsewhere, some individuals have God-given gifts that allow them to play the game better than others. We can't all be Tiger Woods, or Picasso, or Shakespeare, but anybody can learn how to play golf, or paint, or write a sonnet, and we can all learn how to be financially self-sufficient as well."

Let me add again, I agree wholeheartedly that you can learn what you don't know in order to become successful. As you read through these pages, it is my hope that the entrepreneurial stories inside this book help you expand your thinking in your own life and entrepreneurial ventures.

THE LESSONS:

◆ *Be willing to take risks.*

◆ *If you're an entrepreneur, it's inevitable that you'll eventually be the only one who believes in a decision you've got to make. That means you've got to go against the grain and take risks.*

◆ *Entrepreneurs are willing to bet on themselves.*

ENTREPRENEURIAL
REFLECTIONS

2

FIND A WAY

Sometimes things don't always go as you planned. My Dad had a major financial setback shortly before I went to college. The arrival of television devastated his small town movie theater business, so starting college at the age of 16 and financing my higher education often called for some creativity. My plan to pay for college started when I was 14. My family was living in Omaha, and I began searching for a summer job around town. After a frustrating day of rejections, I finally gave up and went to the movie. I sat down next to a girl about my age, and we began talking. I told her about my love of horses, and she told me about riding every summer at the nearby YWCA Camp Brewster. I thanked her, left the theater, and in less than an hour was sitting at the YWCA office talking with the director.

Camp Brewster was owned by, and run for half the summer by, the YWCA. The remainder of the summer the Jewish Community Center leased and operated the facility. I got a job from the YWCA working in the horsemanship program and spent the first half of the summer as the only guy at an all-girls camp. While working at the YWCA camp, I contacted the Jewish Community Center and was hired to work for their riding program the second half of the summer as the only Gentile on the camp staff. Fortunately, they had not been able to find a Jewish Cowboy.

The second year, I was allowed to provide three of the horses each organization leased for the riding program. After my third year, I contracted to direct the horsemanship program and provide all the horses. My summer earnings at Camp Brewster and the JCC camp provided a significant portion of the funds necessary for me to attend college.

I started college in the fall following high school graduation and attended the University of Iowa. My plan called for carrying 20-21 hours a semester and to graduate in 7 semesters with no summer classes. I also needed to work about 30 hours a week while in school, so it was important to get all my classes in the mornings. This allowed me to work in the afternoons and evenings. To get all of my classes in the morning, creative thinking was required. Because registration times were assigned on a rotating basis each semester and further because the morning classes filled up first, I knew that somehow I had to be at the front of the line each semester regardless of that semester's alphabetical registration criteria. I showed up for my first semester's registration early carrying a tray I had liberated from the dorm's cafeteria and dressed in a sports coat and tie even though I didn't meet that semester's criteria for early registration. Fortunately this was before computers took over all our lives. I located the coffee concession outside the secure registration area and bought a half dozen donuts and ten cups of coffee. With the tray loaded and my hands full, I headed for the staff entry gate.

The guard cleared the way and opened the gate for me. After I had been waved through by the gatekeeper, I passed out the coffee and pastries and proceeded to register for all of my classes. I used that same gimmick to register first every semester except the two that alphabetically put me at the front of the line. I never had a class that wasn't over by 1:00 p.m. in my entire college career.

While living in a dormitory at the University, one day I noticed a well-dressed man in the lobby posting a sign on our dorm bulletin board. When he left, I walked over to the board. His sign announced that the tobacco company R.J. Reynolds needed a part-time helper to distribute sample tobacco products in dorms, sororities, and fraternities on campus. The sign said that he would be back in the dorm lobby at 4:00 p.m. the following Wednesday to interview applicants for the position. After looking over my shoulder, I removed the ad from the bulletin board. At 3:30 p.m. the following Wednesday, I replaced the sign on the bulletin board and appeared at 4:00 p.m. for the only interview. Amazingly, I got the job, and I spent the next three years distributing all over campus the freshest four-to-a-pack, wax-sealed cigarettes in existence.

I also worked part-time for an auto repair company aptly named "You Smash 'Em, We Fix 'Em." We had three wreckers we called Baby Bear, Mama Bear and Papa Bear. Papa Bear could pick up and haul anything on the road, and I had an anxious night or two hauling tractor-trailer rigs. The slow night shifts and weekends were great times to study while waiting for the phone to ring. I worked about 30 hours a week there. I soon learned that there was money to be made in wrecked cars. Any time a student or faculty car was brought in with a broken front windshield, I removed the section of glass containing the campus parking permit from the windshield, methodically and carefully removed the sticker from the glass, and put it on a plastic sheet. There was a strong market for those stickers.

The University of Iowa's football coach, Forest Evashevski, produced great teams with a strong fan following. Scalping game tickets also contributed to my education and finances.

In those days, hospitals would buy your blood. But they would only buy your blood once every eight weeks. However, there were two hospitals in Iowa City. I was therefore able to "donate" every four weeks for $15 a pint at one hospital and $25 a pint at the other hospital. Yes, in those days I may have been a little too Machiavellian, but when the objective, in this case a college degree, is important enough, you simply do what you have to do.

During my sixth semester, I was called into the Dean of Students' office. Someone had figured out that I had been forging an advisor's signature for the sign-off on my over 18- hour schedule. I finally convinced the dean that it had been working well for a long time and if I had to drop any hours, I could not graduate in seven semesters and would therefore have to drop out to earn more money. I did graduate after seven semesters - two months before I turned 20.

Just for the record, I stayed busy but had a hell of a lot of fun at college.

Entrepreneurs are willing to do the things others won't do for a few years so that they can do the things others can't do for the rest of their lives.

THE LESSON:

◆ *Entrepreneurs do what it takes to accomplish the goal.*

ENTREPRENEURIAL
REFLECTIONS

3

BE UNIQUE

As college graduation approached, I spent a lot of time preparing for on-campus interviews. I was completing college in seven semesters without summer school and was graduating in January. This meant there were fewer companies interviewing on campus than was the case for spring graduations. The two job offers that I was seriously considering when the interviews ended were with AT&T and Eastman Kodak. I still remember the AT&T interviewer, a very fine gentleman named Otto Stuck. Mr. Stuck said, "Jay, I'm going to make you a job offer despite the fact that I firmly believe that within seven or eight years you'll be in the entrepreneurial world of small business."

The Kodak interviewer had left me with a form to fill out and suggested I accompany the form with a personal letter. In 1960, Kodak was riding high, had 40,000 employees worldwide, and was considered one of the best career opportunities available. I knew that my first impression would be of paramount importance, and that my first impression would of necessity be made by the transmittal letter accompanying my application to the company.

I decided on a go-for-broke approach. At the top of the letter and in capital letters, I typed, "I CAN BRING MORE TO KODAK THAN A COLLEGE EDUCATION." The opening line read, "While operating the south end of a north-bound pitchfork, I had a great deal of time for meditation." The letter went on to explain how, at age 14, I was a stable hand for both the YWCA's Camp Brewster south of Omaha, Nebraska and the Jewish Community Center's camp at the same location the second half of the summer. By the last two summers in college, I furnished all the horses, instruction, and staff for both camps' riding programs. I went on to underline the statement, "I built a barn," and told how the camp needed a larger barn and that the YWCA thought that, since the JCC camp was double the attendance of the Y, the JCC should pay for it. The JCC felt the Y should pay for it because they owned the property. I was able to negotiate a compromise where the two organizations shared the cost, and it was a win for all concerned.

I knew the letter would definitely get a reaction; I just wasn't sure if it would be good or bad. I was ecstatic when Kodak offered me one of only six slots in their two-year executive training program and told me that the advertising department had agreed to pick up my salary for the two years of the program. For the next two years, I floated from department to department, worked directly with top management in each setting, enjoyed working the Kodak pavilion at the New York World Fair for three months, spent time working with the J Walter Thompson Advertising Agency in New York City, and traveled extensively with the sales training department. In those days, Kodak sponsored the highly successful *Ed Sullivan TV Show*. I was not a big fan of Ed Sullivan's, but I learned one thing from him that I have never forgotten, and it has served me well. "Always put your best act on first."

After completing the program, I worked briefly in the advertising department and then took a leave of absence to complete my, at that time, mandatory military service.

Not long after returning to my job with Kodak at their Rochester, NY headquarters, I maneuvered a transfer to Kodak's 10-state Southwest Regional office in Dallas, TX.

Otto Stuck was right. Seven and a half years later, having transferred to Dallas with Kodak, I turned in my resignation and opened Ranchland.

THE LESSONS:

♦ *It may take a few trial and error moments before you figure out what makes you stand out. Leverage your unique difference. Don't go along with the herd because you won't stand out in the crowd. Find ways that make you different in every situation you go into.*

♦ *Be different – when you play to win big, you won't win them all, but you won't get lost in the crowd.*

ENTREPRENEURIAL
REFLECTIONS

4

BET ON PEOPLE

While at Kodak, I joined the military knowing that with my lottery number, I would be drafted anyway. I did a six-month stint on active duty in the Army and then joined a National Guard unit and did one weekend each month and two weeks each summer for the next six years to complete my obligations. I was stationed by the Army for most of my six months' active duty at Fort Sill, near Lawton, Oklahoma. Roy, one of my Kodak customer contacts, lived in Oklahoma City, and I spent many weekends as a guest of Roy and his wife. After my Army service ended and I had transferred to Dallas with Kodak, Roy called to ask if I had $10,000 to invest in an oil deal he was going to invest in. I had $6,000 which I had saved to build a house in the country north of Dallas, but I wanted to invest with Roy. My bank agreed to loan me the additional $4,000. By the time I was to write my check, Roy's driller had already struck oil. I took the drilling logs to the bank, and the bank agreed to lend me the entire $10,000 for my investment. I preserved intact the $6,000 dedicated for the down-payment on my house.

I received royalty checks on that oil well for over 40 years, and to this day I have never even seen the well.

A few years ago, I decided to travel to Southwestern Wyoming with two of my horses and ride in the desert surrounding Little America, where I had lived during my youth. Because I was taking my horses, I called ahead to the local sheriff's department, got the sheriff on the line, and asked for his advice concerning where I might board my horses while there.

He gave me the name of the foreman of the Broad Bent Ranch, and I called Dale. Dale agreed to stable my horses and provide a hook-up at the ranch for my horse trailer with living quarters. After I arrived and settled in, and not wanting to overstep my welcome, I asked Dale if there were any places I should avoid. Dale responded, "I don't think that's a problem. The ranch is a million acres, and we're standing right in the middle of it." Enough said. Over the coming days, I came to greatly respect Dale's knowledge of ranching and horses. When I was leaving, I told him that I was looking to buy two horses, and, if he ran across a couple he thought I might like, I would appreciate him buying them for me. Some weeks later, I received a call from Dale.

He had purchased two horses for me at a total cost of less than $2,000. I told him I would make arrangements for their shipment to Texas. Once I had received an $836 quote for the shipment, I called Dale and offered to pay that amount of money to him if he and his wife wanted a short vacation in Texas. He did, and he and his wife spent some time with Bettye and me at our home in rural North Texas. My neighbors were more than impressed with Dale's judgment of horseflesh. After I initially resisted, I sold one of the horses for $6,000 and ten years later sold the other one for $18,750. I was willing to take Dale's horses sight unseen because I had bet on Dale, and I received a sizable return on my bet as my reward. Oh yes, I did send Dale a thank-you note with a $1,000 check enclosed.

When I transferred to Dallas with Kodak, I had an assistant named Shirley. Shirley and her husband were originally from the rural Quitman, Texas area, and both sets of their parents still lived there. Shirley and her husband wanted to buy land near Quitman that in time they could build on and retire. To that end, they spent most weekends traveling to Quitman and looking at available real estate. One Monday morning, I walked in to the office to find Shirley, not certain if she was excited or depressed. It seems that over the weekend she and her husband had finally found the ideal piece of property, a 100-acre tract in two parcels separated by a road through the property. Eighty acres lay on one side of the road, and twenty acres lay on the other side. Unfortunately, the owner would only sell the entire 100-acre tract. He was willing to take 20% down and a long term note at a very fair interest rate. Shirley and spouse, even stretching to their limit, could only afford the 80-acre parcel. Shirley was perplexed and asked if I had any thoughts as to a solution to their problem. I said, "Shirley! You don't have a problem. I will buy the 20 acres. The seller will be happy to sell the parcels separately as long as they close simultaneously and he doesn't have to worry about ending up with one parcel. What's more, I want you to understand that I am not doing you a favor. You are doing me one."

Shirley was aghast. "You haven't even seen the property," she said.

"I know," I responded. "But you've been looking at real estate in that area most every weekend for months, both of your families know land values there, road frontage adds value, and the twenty acres has four times as much frontage per acre as the eighty. Rural land in large parcels typically sells for less money per acre than it does in small parcels. You will get the land you want, and I will have a great investment."

The seller was happy to take our separate notes as long as we did a simultaneous closing assuring that the entire one hundred acres sold at the same time. Shirley had her dream property. I didn't even see the property until a year later. When I sold less than two years later, the buyer found me. I paid no commission and sold for more than double my purchase price. And, I will always be Shirley's white knight.

THE LESSON:

◆ *You do not always need all the facts or eyes-on the investment to make the right decisions. In order to win, bet on winners. In most transactions, you are betting primarily on people. Follow your gut feelings.*

5

JUDGE NOT
LEST YE BE JUDGED

Having maneuvered a transfer from Kodak's headquarters in Rochester, NY to Dallas, TX, I began making preparations to relocate. I called my friend George, the Kodak advertising representative with whom I would share responsibility for the 10 state southwest region. George asked, "Does your car have air conditioning?"

Although I was the proud owner of a sporty Thunderbird, I had to answer, "No."

George responded, "You will never be able to sell a luxury car in Texas if it isn't air-conditioned." My promotion included a company car when I got to Texas but I had planned to drive my Thunderbird to Texas, and then sell it. I needed to sell my car while still in New York.

From that moment forward, I asked every single person I encountered, "Do you want to buy a Thunderbird?" I even prepared a selling sheet that I carried with me and handed out.

I had begun to fear that I would have to accept a low wholesale offer I had received for my car and ship my personal possessions to Texas. Three nights before I was scheduled to leave for Dallas, I went to the laundromat about midnight to do some laundry. When I walked in, the janitor was mopping the floor. As I had done with every other person I had encountered, I said, "Would you like to buy a Thunderbird?"

He stopped mopping, leaned on his mop, and said, "I have always wanted to own a Thunderbird."

He drove a Golden Hawk Studebaker that the highway department's ice and snow control chemicals had almost rusted to the ground. I had padded my asking price by about $400. So, I allowed him $400 for his car and we closed the deal the next day.

Two days later, I loaded all my possessions in the Studebaker and headed for Texas with Kodak paying me 12¢ a mile.

I could see the highway through the floorboards, and every hundred miles I had to add brake fluid through another opening in the floorboard. While I had doubts about whether his car would make it from New York to Dallas, I figured that I could always push it into the ditch and catch the bus. I made it all the way to Dallas in that Studebaker and pocketed Kodak's 12¢ a mile. I picked up my company car and sold the Studebaker for $20.

THE LESSON:

◆ *Don't judge a book by its cover. Be open to opportunity and ready to sell or buy from anyone because you never know who the buyer or seller may be. The truth is, everyone is a buyer, and everyone is a seller. Sometimes taking a risk involves a great adventure. The life of an entrepreneur is always, always an adventure!*

ENTREPRENEURIAL
REFLECTIONS

6

REAL ESTATE

When I transferred with Kodak to Dallas, after settling in the first thing I did was buy a horse. I boarded my horse in what was then still a somewhat rural area on the north edge of Dallas close to Addison Airport. When I went to ride one weekend morning, the owner of the property where I boarded my horse told me he was about to go look at a nearby 11-acre piece of property he was thinking about buying. When he invited me to go along, I accepted. The tract contained a house, servant quarters that hadn't been occupied for several years, a horse-barn, a separate stud barn, a lighted arena, and an 8N Ford tractor used to mow the property. In short, a nice piece of property. A few weeks later I asked my friend what had come of his efforts to buy that property. He informed me that he had decided not to pursue the purchase. I immediately went over, talked to the owner, and discovered that the owner wanted $76,000 for the land, buildings, tractor and all (1966 pricing). Because I was young and had no money, I began to plan how I could come up with the down payment.

I contacted my dad, who a few years earlier had narrowly avoided bankruptcy in the theater business that had been rendered unprofitable by the arrival of television in rural Iowa. Dad wrote me a poignant letter indicating that he was pleased to be able to help me at a time in my young life when his help would still be meaningful. He mortgaged his just paid off $16,000 home for the $12,000 I needed. It's an enormous advantage in life to have someone who believes in you. I knew that no matter what happened, I could make the $83.96 monthly payments on his loan.

I then called my close friend at Kodak, George, and told him I had located a property that we needed to buy, and he agreed to go 50/50 and put up his $12,000. George and I began a series of unsuccessful efforts with local lenders and banks to secure the loan necessary for us to buy the property. After still another failed attempt, I optimistically told George that I thought we should call our new property the GJ Ranch, with "G" standing for George and "J" standing for me. George said: "I like it, because if this doesn't work I can always say, 'Gee, Jay, how did we get ourselves into this mess?'"

We finally secured our loan and closed on the property. I cleaned up the long abandoned servant's quarters and moved in to cut my expenses. The rent we received on the main house almost covered our mortgage payments. Eighteen months later, we sold the property for $200,000. Our profit was the seed money for a still larger dream: Ranchland.

THE LESSON:

◆ *Don't overlook real estate as a great way to make money.*

ENTREPRENEURIAL
REFLECTIONS

7

MAKE A MOVE

The one who makes the most moves often wins because as the saying goes, you can't make any of the shots you don't take. You can't win if you don't make a move. Entrepreneurs are always thinking and always taking action.

Once I had some capital and a regular Kodak paycheck, I began to pursue my dream of owning acreage away from the city where I worked. A fellow member of the Shriners' Black Horse Patrol who lived northwest of Dallas invited me and my horse out to ride one weekend. When I arrived, he was finishing a project, so I decided to ride out alone for a while. As I was riding, I approached a stock pond and there encountered a man in bib overalls with a two-day growth of beard, a fishing pole, and a beer. As I got closer, he said, "That's about the prettiest horse I ever saw. I'll trade you this fishing pole for your horse." I figured he was a local hired hand, and without another word spoken, I dismounted, took his fishing pole and his beer, and he rode off on my horse. He returned about thirty minutes later and exclaimed that he had not been on a horse in over twenty years and had never been on one that was so well mannered or handled so smoothly.

We struck up a conversation, and I learned that he owned 240 acres, including the land we were standing on. I told him my friend had a few acres near him, and I was looking to buy land in the area. We agreed that next Saturday I would bring two horses and we would ride over his land together. My parting words were, "When we ride out of your woods next weekend, I want to own some of your land."

The following Saturday when our ride was over, I did. Specifically, it was an 80-acre tract that was somewhat set apart from his other land. I agreed to purchase the 80 acres for $72,000, 70% of which he agreed to carry on a note. I carved out the back 10 acres for my homestead and sold the remaining 70 acres in 2-1/2 to 15 acre tracts so quickly that I was able to pay off his note in less than a year. I then began work on the house that I had been building in my mind for many years.

Yes, I was extra lucky, but even if the fisherman had been a local hired hand, I could have learned a lot from him. Much like selling my Thunderbird to the janitor…don't prejudge people.

THE LESSON:

- *Keep the momentum going. Always learn, be proactive, and be willing to make a move.*

8

GET CREATIVE

One weekend when I was out working at my house's construction site, a neighbor who I had not met but owned the ranch adjacent to my property, came by. He introduced himself as Bob and asked how the project was coming along. He invited me to have dinner with him and his wife. "I'm hot and dirty," I said.

He said that I was his size and that he would lay some clothes out in the cabana at their pool. I decided to go. Some of the best decisions are last minute. I jumped into the pool, cooled down, took a quick shower, dressed, and joined them for dinner.

Bob told me over dinner how he had been the number two man at the Southwest Division of Sears, and he had been operating this ranch as his transition into retirement. He was now ready to sell his 165-acre ranch, move with his wife to Sedona, Arizona, and really retire. He was asking $330,000 for the ranch. (Money was worth a great deal more in the 1960s).

The ranch had a magnificent ranch house complete with pool and cabana, a clean modern two-bedroom foreman's house, and an outstanding horse barn with a finished-out office, a covered porch, ten box stalls, and many amenities. The property also had two smaller out-buildings and a huge hay barn.

Because he saw me as a kid and not as a prospective buyer, he confided in me that, if necessary, he would throw in his herd of thirty mother cows with calves by their side, two tractors, the farm equipment, and a pickup truck. When I casually inquired, Bob told me he wanted a solid deal so he would have to get $50,000 down, but he would be happy to carry a 6% note for the $280,000 balance.

When I thanked Alice and Bob Carr (ABC Ranch) for a lovely meal and evening, I was trying to play it calm and cool, but my head was spinning. I got to town about 9:00 p.m. and immediately grabbed a legal pad and pen. Sometimes you have to get creative, especially if you don't have capital. By 2 a.m., I had laid out the business plan for the ranch. Additionally, I had a three-page list of potential investors who consisted primarily of my fellow Kodak employees and my Kodak customers. The ranch would host corporate convention groups, company meetings, and employee picnics. For two four-week sessions each year, the ranch would be exclusively devoted to a youth horsemanship program.

My business plan called for raising $170,000 to make the down payment, build the bunk houses, launch the business, and reach cash flow positive.

Three nights after my dinner with Bob and Alice, with money raised, I knocked on their door, contract in hand. The Carrs were, to say the least, shocked. A rumor was soon circulating among the locals that some young kid had lost his mind and paid $2,000 per acre for 165 acres. (Less improvements, cattle, and personal property, I figured it was about $1,200 per acre.)

Today, 48 years later, land in this area is selling from a low of $60,000 per acre to a high of over $100,000 per acre.

In any event, my dream of Ranchland had become reality. But it wouldn't have happened if I hadn't gotten creative in finding solutions to buy it.

THE LESSON:

◆ *Entrepreneurs always find a different way. Sometimes it's not the normal way or the way everyone else does it, but they find a way to make things happen in their favor.*

ENTREPRENEURIAL
REFLECTIONS

9

ASK AND
YE SHALL RECEIVE

After I raised the money to buy Ranchland, my youth summer ranch/horsemanship venture and corporate dude ranch, my next challenge was making the youngsters (and, more importantly, their parents) aware of its existence and signing them up for one or both of two 4-week summer sessions. I had little money for marketing and public relations. Time was running short and enrollments were coming far too slowly. Sitting at my desk contemplating my first major failure and bankruptcy at the ripe old age of 28, I was flipping through the *Western Horseman* magazine (the world's most popular and widely-circulated horse magazine at that time), and noticed the magazine's masthead. It listed Dick Spencer, III as publisher along with the magazine's address in Colorado Springs, CO and phone number. On impulse, I picked up the phone and dialed the number. When the receptionist answered, I asked to speak to Mr. Spencer. Lo' and behold, I was connected, and a pleasant voice said, "What can I do for you?"

I said, "Mr. Spencer, I'm opening a summer youth horsemanship ranch north of Dallas/Ft. Worth and am coming to Colorado Springs to take you to lunch and tell you about it. I called to find out when you would like me to be there."

ASK and you shall receive. We had lunch the following week. The magazine did a color spread followed by numerous continued columns and a total of sixteen pictures.

As a result of the article, our summer youth ranch was a booming success and enrolled boys and girls from thirty-eight states. That fall, Dick sent the editor, Chuck King, down to participate in a four-day extended weekend adult horsemanship course we offered. His attendance generated another great article that helped fill several adult horsemanship clinics. The corporate dude ranch/meeting facility we operated the other ten months of the year also became very successful, and I was able to remove bankruptcy from my list of upcoming events.

The principle of "ask and ye shall receive" served me well during the marketing and building of Ranchland.

Most of my Ranchland investors and the board of directors were former fellow employees of Kodak and Kodak customers. These were friends with whom I had close relationships.

At a board meeting, I read a draft of the copy I had prepared for the youth ranch brochure. When I read that Jim Shoulders, 16-time World Champion Rodeo cowboy, would visit the ranch during each of the two sessions to personally meet and visit with the youngsters, one of the board members who fully appreciated Jim's fame and celebrity status stopped me and said, "Jay, how in the world did you get Jim Shoulders to agree to come to the ranch?"

I answered, "I haven't. In fact, I've never met or spoken to the man, but I think his presence and endorsement will be a major plus, and I'm sure going to try to make it happen."

The following week, I called Jim at his Oklahoma ranch. He agreed to visit with me, and I drove up for the meeting. Jim agreed not only to visit each session at the ranch, but to also attend the press party that announced our summer youth horsemanship program and our corporate offerings to the DFW market. His presence ensured us a great turnout. Knowing that we were a struggling startup, Jim refused to accept any compensation for his support. In those days, even the top rodeo cowboys didn't make big money. Thanks to Jim, over seventy members of the media attended, and we received outstanding coverage.

There are a lot of nice people out there and a lot of people who are willing to be helpful, but they can't say "yes" if you don't ask them. If you're not good at asking for things, maybe you need to be.

I was very gratified a few years later to learn that Jim had been in an incredibly successful Miller Beer TV commercial.

When I ran into my friend Neil Gay, the owner of the Mesquite Rodeo in Texas, he told me the details of the Miller Beer TV commercial story.

Jim got a call from an advertising executive in New York City. The exec said, "Jim, I'm calling to see if you would be interested in being in a Miller Beer commercial we're about to produce."

Jim replied that he'd be interested but there were a couple of hurdles they would need to get over. The ad exec asked what those would be. Jim said, "Well, first, there are thousands of young people who look up to me, and I promised myself that I wouldn't take part in anything that wasn't in good taste."

The advertising executive responded that Miller Beer was very sensitive in that area, and he was absolutely certain that it wouldn't be a problem. He assured Jim he would have the right to reject anything he was uncomfortable with. The exec then asked about the second hurdle.

Jim said, "Of course, that would be the money."

The executive explained that the money Jim received would be based on the number of times the commercial was shown in each market and the size of those markets. He concluded by saying, "However, in the event, for whatever reason, we never use the commercial at all, you would receive a check for $12,000."

Jim simply said, "Well, now that we're over that hurdle…"

As it turns out, that commercial was so popular and ran so long that Jim's compensation for that one commercial was greater than several years of his rodeo income, if not all of it.

A much more recent but excellent example of the power of asking is the story of getting acquainted with Norm Brodsky, co-author of *Street Smarts*.

I had intended to entitle this book *Street Smarts*. Much to my cha-grin, as I was looking for material for the Biz Owners' Ed program, I came across a book by Norm Brodsky titled *Street Smarts*. I was upset that my title had been stolen but ordered a copy of the book. The book is directed at entrepreneurs starting and growing their busi-nesses. It proved to be the very best book for business owners that I have ever read. I doubt that a better one exists. I was so excited by the clarity and conciseness of the lessons it teaches that I ordered 150 copies for the Biz Owners' Ed program and put meeting the author at the top of my to-do list.

My assistant Cari worked her magic and came up with Mr. Brodsky's phone number. When I got him on the phone, we visited and I told him that I very much wanted to take him to lunch. "With you living in Texas and me in New York City, just when and where do you want to do that?" he asked.

"Absolutely anywhere and anytime that's convenient for you," I replied.

Entrepreneurs have to be ready for opportunity. Sometimes it doesn't knock twice.

Three weeks later, Biz Owners' Ed co-founder David Hammer and I flew to New York City, met Mr. Brodsky at his condominium next door to Donald's Trump Tower and enjoyed an incredible two and a half hour lunch soaking up Norm's wisdom. In the process, I asked Norm if he would be willing to say a few words at the annual Biz Owners' Ed alumni luncheon in June and be the speaker for the Dallas Entrepreneurs' Organization dinner the following night at the

George W. Bush Library. As frequently happens when you ask, Norm graciously accepted the invitation. Both of Norm's presentations were outstanding. He drew the biggest crowd Dallas Entrepreneurs' Organization had attracted all year, blew away the attendees at our Biz Owners' Ed luncheon, and presented Biz Owners' Ed with a $5,000 donation check thus becoming our first out-of-state mentor.

THE LESSON:

◆ **ASK.**

This chapter contains only three of the hundreds, if not thousands, of wonderful happenings that have occurred throughout my personal and professional life simply because I always ask.

10

UNDERSTAND THE
COST OF A SINGLE INVESTOR

I f you've got a fantastic business idea and someone else agrees, it sure can be tempting to take their money and sell shares or bring them on as an investor in order to build it. Most entrepreneurs don't have sufficient savings to adequately capitalize their first business. I was no exception. However, I resisted the temptation to land the big single investor with all the capital I would ever need. I resisted because the Golden Rule of Business is, "He who has the gold makes the rules."

Instead, I decided to raise the necessary capital from several investors. I limited the amount of money that each single investor could contribute so that there would be no "first among equals." I ensured that I would not start with multiple shareholders in a single voting block attributable to pre-existing relationships among them by making sure that my personal relationships with each investor was solid.

I implemented that effort at shareholder diversity, and I remained in charge of my business and in control of my own destiny from date of formation until the date we sold. Don't create the circumstances under which your shareholders can run you out of your own company by taking the easy way out in raising money from a single investor or a group of related investors. I have seen it happen many times.

When I started Ranchland, my investors owned 80% and I owned 20%. They were putting something at risk. I was risking everything and wanted some control of my destiny. Today, that could be accomplished with an LLC, which was not an option in the 1960s. My answer was setting up a Sub-S corporation. I got all voting stock, and the investors got both voting and non-voting stock in a ratio that gave the entire investor group 55% of the vote and I had 45%. I explained to them that, whereas they were only putting up money, I was putting my future on the line. However, because I respected them and their business acumen, if they nearly all disagreed with me, they might even be right and their vote could prevail. The ideal investor can contribute more to your company than just money. Expertise (lawyers, CPAs), advice, and contacts are a few of the extras your investors will hopefully bring along with their money.

THE LESSON:

♦ *Don't rush into accepting investor money. Think carefully about the structure of the deal and avoid getting locked-in to one investor. If you do something for the money now, you might regret it later on. Your ideal investors will bring more to the table than just money.*

11

DIVIDE AND MULTIPLY

My Ranchland property was half a mile north of Farm to Market 1171 near Roanoke, TX, a paved, secondary east-west thoroughfare north of Dallas/Ft. Worth. Many visitors experienced difficulty in finding the backroad entrance to the Ranch. I wanted Ranchland to have an entrance directly off of F.M. 1171, so I went about looking at adjacent properties that did in fact front on F.M. 1171.

One such property was a 100-acre tract divided by F.M. 1171 into two parcels, 65 acres north of F.M. 1171 on the same side as Ranchland, and 35 acres on the south side of FM1171. I searched the deed records and eventually found out that the 100 acres were owned by 21 heirs of the original owner and that all but one of those heirs lived out-of-state. The one Texas heir lived only 15 minutes from the Ranch. I called the largest heir who lived in Arizona and learned that he could speak for most of the heirs and would in fact be willing to sell for $2,000 an acre; however, because so many heirs were involved, it had to be an all-cash sale. My cash position was approximately zero. The one local heir, I dubbed him

"Roanoke Willie," had been looking after the property for his relatives. I didn't have $200,000 and wasn't even certain that I could borrow $200,000, but I continued to think about that property and the Ranchland access I needed.

One day, I noticed a man with a tractor out working the property. I stopped to talk. It turned out that he was paying Willie to rent the 100 acres. He was a local farmer whom Roanoke Willie had promised 5% of the proceeds of any sale as compensation for the erosion control the farmer had put in place on the property. Because I knew from the primary heir that Roanoke Willie only owned 1% or 2%, I was confident that he had no ability or intention to perform on his promise of 5% of any sales proceeds. I also quietly determined that the other heirs were unaware of Willie's promise to his tenant. Additionally, Roanoke Willie was not sharing the proceeds of the rent he was collecting. I made these points to the local farmer and offered him $2,500 to release any and all claims he might have if I was able to buy the property. He understood the situation and agreed to the $2,500.

I had previously noticed a large estate adjacent on the east side of the property and on the same side of F.M. 1171 as Ranchland. The owner, Gary Levitz, was the heir to, and the successful-in-his-own-right operator of, the Levitz retail furniture chain. My banker Walter knew Gary and agreed to arrange a lunch meeting to introduce us.

I then developed a plan. Working with the primary heir, I entered into two contracts, in the name of Jay D. Rodgers and/or assigns. (Never make an offer on real estate without adding "and/or assigns" to the name of the buyer.) One contract was for the 65 acres north of F.M. 1171 at $2,600+ an acre, and the second contract was for the 35 acres south of F.M. 1171 at $886+ an acre. The 35-acre contract had a provision requiring the 65-acre contract to be funded before I could close on the smaller tract. This assured the sellers of receiving their full asking price of $2,000 an acre for the 100 acres. A couple of days after the two contracts had been signed, I met my banker and Gary for lunch.

At lunch, I told Gary about my two contracts and that trying to close on both would stretch me. I told him that the 65 acres immediately to the west of his magnificent estate would be an attractive addition to his holdings. He agreed and asked me what I wanted for that contract. I told him that I wanted a road easement to Ranchland down the far west side of his soon-to-be new holding and a check for $5,000 to assign the 65-acre contract to him. He agreed on the spot, and three weeks later, Gary closed on the 65 acres. Gary could, and did, pay cash for that property. I paid the farmer $2,500 out of Gary's $5,000 and gave the banker the remaining $2,500 for setting up the luncheon with Gary.

After my lunch with Gary, I had called two former Kodak customers, told them in detail exactly what I had done, and offered to sell each 1/3 of the 35 acre tract for $20,000 each. At that point, I had spent over a year on the deal, and land value had been going straight up. The fair market was between $2,500 and $3,000 an acre. They both jumped on my offer. When the dust settled, the ranch had an entrance on FM 1171, I owned 1/3 of the 35 acres free and clear, and I had received cash of over $8,000 at the closing.

Thank goodness I did not limit my thinking to just acquiring an easement. Sometimes it's just better to buy more than what you want in order to end up with what you want.

P.S. Today (40+ years later), the land in that area starts at $60,000 an acre.

THE LESSON:

◆ *Look for opportunities to divide and multiply. One simple deal might just contain a whole lot more than you think. Look at all sides of the transaction.*

ENTREPRENEURIAL REFLECTIONS

ENTREPRENEURIAL
REFLECTIONS

"PAYCHECKS ARE ADDICTIVE

AND A MAJOR HINDRANCE

TO BUILDING WEALTH."

JAY D. RODGERS

12

ASK! THEY MAY RECONSIDER

S ometimes you shouldn't believe what others tell you about their bottom lines, or about the bottom lines of other people. My partner Darrell and I frequented a coffee shop in Denton where the locals got together to enjoy morning coffee and exchange stories (swap lies). At one of those sessions, we heard a tale about a local builder we knew named Joe who badly needed to sell an auto repair shop he owned and was leasing to a local mechanic. Times were hard in the real estate business, and interest rates were in excess of 18%. Joe was in a liquidity crunch. The locals were adamant that Joe was selling the building way too cheap, but the deal had to be 100% cash at closing, and no one had that much cash.

Darrell and I believed that we could borrow the money necessary to buy Joe's property. Our bank looked at our proposal and agreed to lend all but $15,000 of the money needed. We went to Joe and told him we would buy his property but that he would have to carry a $15,000 second lien note that would be subordinate to the bank's first lien note. Joe agreed. (Ask and you shall receive). Joe had previously received a deposit and the last month's rent from his tenant. Those funds were deducted at closing from Joe's proceeds and credited to us. Darrell and I walked away from the closing with the deed and a $2,300 check in our pocket. Neither Darrell nor I ever put a single penny of our own money into this income property. We sold it three years later for a handsome profit. Never take someone else's word about another's requirements to make a deal

When Bettye and I had a company called Healthcare Staff Resources, we often had a healthcare professional who would ask us to mark their profile indicating that they would not work Thursday shifts or some other specific time. My instructions were that if we were having trouble filling a shift, disregard the notation. You would not believe the number of shifts we filled with people that had indicated they were not available for those specific hours.

THE LESSON:

♦ *No one says "yes" to a question that you do not ask.*

13

GIVE YOURSELF A GIFT

Have you ever done a deal with someone you didn't feel good about? Trust those instincts, and don't let greed or money cause you to do business with people you don't respect.

During the early years I owned Ranchland, a farrier by the name of B. R. Blagg shod my horses. One day when he was not scheduled to shoe horses at my place, he showed up with a black horse. He knew I was a member of the Dallas Hella Temple Shriners Black Horse Patrol, and black horses that met the Patrol's requirements were hard to find. Because I had a ranch near Dallas, many of the Patrol members asked for my assistance when they needed a horse.

B.R. showed me his horse, and I immediately knew it had a better chance of being a dog's dinner than a Shriner's Patrol horse. I didn't let on that I was shocked that he would present such a horse to me. Back in the 60s, we were routinely paying from $2,500-$5,000 for our mounts in the Patrol. I was sure that at the local auction his horse would sell by the pound and bring $300-$400. B.R. told me he was asking $3,500 for the horse. I said, "B.R., I want you to load up your horse, get off my property and never come back." Totally shocked and perhaps thinking about the immediate loss of a portion of his far-rier's revenue, he asked why. I told him that I couldn't afford to have anyone around me who thought so little of me as to try to sell me a $400 horse for $3,500. If you deal with a skunk long enough, you are bound to get sprayed.

This experience prompted me to receive a gift I've enjoyed throughout my business life. It was a gift I gave myself. I vowed that in the future I would not do business with anyone that I didn't respect and somewhat enjoy being around. The gift has definitely made my business life much more enjoyable, and I personally believe it has made my business dealings more financially rewarding. Life is short. Life is more fun if you surround yourself with business associates you respect, trust, and enjoy working with. All the great deals I have ever done have happened with extremely smart people on the other side of the table. Winning a deal 51 to 49 is not near as much fun as losing 59 to 61 because smart, win-win entrepreneurs figure out how to add 20 points to the total value.

THE LESSONS:

- *Life is short.*

- *Life is more fun if you surround yourself with business associates you respect, trust, and enjoy working with. All the great deals I have ever done have happened with extremely smart people on the other side of the table. Winning a deal 51 to 49 is not near as much fun as losing 59 to 61 because smart, win-win entrepreneurs figure out how to add 20 points to the total value.*

ENTREPRENEURIAL
REFLECTIONS

14

UNDERSTAND
WHAT MOTIVATES
PEOPLE YOU DEAL WITH

O ne of the best traits of successful entrepreneurs is the ability to judge people and their motivations and to understand what makes them tick. During my Ranchland days, I spent a considerable amount of money on direct mail. I used direct mail pieces to attract both youngsters to my summer youth ranch program and corporations for my corporate dude ranch and meeting facilities. The closest post office to Ranchland was 15 minutes away in the rural community of Roanoke, Texas. The post office building occupied less than 1,000 square feet. At that time in the late 1960s, the number of stamps a post office sold was a key factor in its rating.

The magnitude of my direct mail operation had a major impact on the little post office in Roanoke. Because of our stamp purchases, the Roanoke post office was allowed to install a telephone which they had not previously been permitted. Additionally, all of the employees except the postmaster received a raise.

I remembered this lesson a few years later when I signed on to help American Health Profiles, working with Farmland Industries and their many Midwestern rural cooperatives to provide mobile multi-phasic health testing to their members. We sent out hundreds of thousands of direct mail pieces promoting the service, and timing was critical to coordinate the mailing with the arrival of the mobile health vans. Because I understood the post office's rating system, I was always able to motivate a postmaster to go above and beyond. AHP could never receive discounted postage or any other sort of financial remuneration for directing its business to a particular post office, nor could we offer additional compensation for accommodating our sometimes frenetic schedule. However, the local postmasters who would stay open late for us and would open the back door for us on Saturday or Sunday if need be were the ones who got our stamp business and mailing volume. It was a great negotiating tool. My understanding is that today the stamp sales revenues are no longer considered in post office ratings, but the volume of mail is.

THE LESSONS:

◆ *The lesson applies to other dealings as well.*
You never learn if or how to deal with someone
in business unless you understand what motivates them
and how to help them achieve their goals. Sometimes
their motivator is something completely different than
what you might expect. Take the time to find out.

◆ *If you can see John Jones through John Jones' eyes,*
you can sell John Jones what John Jones buys.

ENTREPRENEURIAL REFLECTIONS

15

MISTAKES MATTER

The wise man uses mistakes to fuel his future, while the fool looks at a mistake as a failure. Mistakes are a part of life, and the sooner you realize that and glean some valuable lessons from them, the better off you'll be. When I was in my late twenties or early thirties, I decided to get my pilot's license. I went to the FBO at the Denton Airport in Texas and signed up for lessons. While I was there, I met another enrolling student named George. After talking for a while, George and I decided to team up and take our lessons back-to-back so that, when George took his lesson, I could sit behind George and our instructor Bill and listen and learn. When it was my turn, we would simply switch places. This plan worked out great, and we also studied together for our ground school tests.

A few weeks into this arrangement, I arrived for our lessons, and Bill told me that George had called to say that a family situation had come up and he would not be joining us today. Bill and I pre-flighted the plane and flew out west of Denton. When we returned to the airport, our normal routine was to do a few touch-and-goes. As I was on final approach, Bill said, "When you land, just pull over on the taxiway and stop."

When I stopped, Bill informed me that he was getting out and that I was going to solo. I was absolutely astounded. I said, "What do you mean? How can I solo? George hasn't soloed yet, and he makes great landings every time."

His response was, "Jay, you have screwed up nearly every landing and made every mistake known to mankind. You have mastered correcting and recovering. I know that if something goes wrong, you will be able to right it and land safely. Because George always lands perfectly, I have no idea what he will do when he has a problem. Until I do, he is not ready to solo."

My instructor's thinking highlights the value of mentors and coaches. People who have the experience, who "have been there and done that," often see the road ahead more clearly than those of us who are traveling it for the first time.

THE LESSON:

◆   *There is a lot to be said for learning from our mistakes.*

16

PLAN, PREPARE, AND STRATEGIZE

I have always enjoyed playing poker. In my early thirties, I got serious about it for a period of time. Although gambling is technically illegal in Texas, there are several regular poker games that take place. Because my brother-in-law and a close personal friend both owned construction companies, I started playing regularly with a group of contractors. Routinely, their crews got under way by 7 a.m. and they had been up for a couple of hours by then. On game nights, they would rush home after shutting down the crews for the day, grab a quick shower, inhale some dinner, and head to the game. Because it was their night out, they would invariably over indulge in "authority water" while enjoying the comradery.

I, on the other hand, was focused totally on winning. Many of the pots would contain over $500 and pots in excess of $1,000 were not extremely rare. I wasn't then, and have never been, among the world's great poker players, but thanks to numerous strategic advantages, I was a very consistent winner. On game days, I slept late, ate moderately, had an hour or an hour and a half massage, and finished my pre-game mid-afternoon meal a couple of hours before game time. I drank almost nothing prior to and during the game. All in all, those practices gave me a huge advantage at the table.

In applying my belief that if you wanted to win, it was important that you not play with people who were better than you. I kept extremely accurate records of each player's winnings and losses. This allowed me to frequently avoid getting in an expensive head's up situation with the one contractor who consistently won.

I convinced myself that, even though I was perhaps not too far above average as a poker player, with proper preparation, discipline, and procedures I could consistently win. And, with only one or two games a week, I could make a living. Despite that, I stopped playing regularly and for the last forty plus years have played very rarely. The two major factors in deciding to give up playing regularly were:

(1.) By applying the same amount of time and energy, business and investment opportunities were much more rewarding and frequently more fun.

(2.) When I analyzed it, I realized that all the combined time and energy expended by all the players in the game did not produce or create anything. They simply redistributed existing wealth. Therefore, you could only feel good about it if you accepted the fact that it had some recreational value.

THE LESSON:

◆ *You don't need to be the world's greatest hunter to shoot the biggest bear.*

ENTREPRENEURIAL
REFLECTIONS

17

CHANGING THE GAME

As a boy, I always enjoyed pinball machines. My enjoyment of them caused me to think about how the owners of the machines made money with them. I observed the machines in establishments and noticed that the vending machine companies changed out the machines periodically. Because my experience with them caused me to know there was nothing wrong with the machines, I wondered what the reason was for the change and all the effort that change entailed. In observing further, I noticed a correlation between the length of time a machine was present in an establishment and the number of people who played the machine. The longer a machine was there, the less the patrons played it. So, I decided that the most profitable pinball machine business would avoid the expense of frequent rotation of the machines. I concluded that an airport was the ideal place for a pinball concession, because there it's the people who change. There's no need to change the machines.

I acquired the pinball concession at the DFW Airport. Actually, I convinced Dobbs House to let me put a machine in each of their twenty-four cocktail lounges scattered in various DFW terminals. I took half, and they took half. I enjoyed trucking quarters to the bank until I sold the venture at a handsome profit.

THE LESSON:

◆ *Sometimes it's easier and more profitable to change the players than to change the game.*

18

BIGGER ISN'T
NECESSARILY BETTER

For many years, I was an active member of the Dallas Chapter of The CEO Club.

The CEO Club, like many executive organizations, seeks to create peer-to-peer networks of executives so that each member may benefit from the experience and advice of their fellow members. At CEO Club meetings, one member presents his company in-depth, and the other members then present their thoughts, comments, and suggestions.

In those presentations, I noticed a disturbing tendency to focus on gross revenue rather than on bottom-line profit. After one presentation by my friend Aggie, I said, "Aggie, you have laid out a great plan for huge revenue growth over the next three years; however, I did not hear a single reference to Net Income. The Stock Market, through its quoted P/E ratio, and in most cases buyers of small businesses through their use of EBITDA multiples, value companies based upon their bottom lines, not their top lines. As comforting as it is to view growth in revenue numbers, you're misleading yourself if that's the way you're choosing to plan your growth and measure success. Most revenue belongs to other people or companies, and you are required to handle, process, and account for it. Only that small portion of revenue that makes it to the bottom line is yours to spend. Personally, I think your growth plan should be built around growing net profits, and the need to handle more revenue is just one of the unfortunate requirements."

The Lesson:

◆ *Don't let big overshadow profitable.*

19

NEVER BUY A MAN'S NOTE
UNLESS HE WANTS YOU TO

In the late 80s, bank regulators decided that many banks had bad loans and weren't financially solid. The regulators made Texas their first target. Banks that were deemed unsound were closed or sold. Many loans were shipped to major financial institutions in far-off cities. As a result, people who could were often able to buy their loans back for a fraction of the amount owed. Those who couldn't afford to buy their loans were at the mercy of the bank.

The regulators sold weak banks to other sound banks. Banks that bought these banks were given allowances on specific classified loans. To get rid of the bad loans, the banks could sell them at huge discounts and still break even while getting bad loans off of their books and cleaning up their loan portfolios.

I became involved when two brothers came to me for help after their local bank sold and the new owner called in all four of their loans. Their bank had been purchased by the Ford Group that owned several banks. In the course of helping the brothers, I became acquainted with Alan Cawthon, the new president of their bank. Alan told me the bank owned several classified loans.

I looked at the loans that were available for sale and asked Alan if I committed to buy several of the loans, would he be willing to modify the loan terms before I took them. Alan said that wouldn't be a problem as long as the debtors agreed.

I picked out the loans that I wanted and went to each debtor to tell them that I was looking at buying a group of loans from his bank and his loan(s) was one among them. I explained that, per the fine print in their loan documents, their note was a negotiable instrument that the bank could sell without their consent. However, I had a personal rule that I would never buy a person's loan unless he/she wanted me to. I was there to determine if they wanted me to buy their note.

Everyone I visited with was mad at the bank for calling their loans, so it was an easy question. I took it a step further and asked what they didn't like about the terms of the loan and why they would like me to buy it. Some needed longer amortization periods to reduce their monthly payment. Some knew the notes were selling at a discount and wanted the option to pay off the note early at a reduced price. And, some were so upset at the bank that they were happy for me to buy their note(s) with no changes.

In many cases, I revised the amortization schedules to lower monthly payments. In some cases, I agreed to sell them the note later at a discount, or made other adjustments to enlist their support and enthusiasm. I had the bank make all the adjustments so that I didn't have to mess with the paperwork.

Out of the approximately eighty notes I bought at between 20% and 70% of their face value, I never lost a single cent on any note including two instances where we later agreed on a deed in-lieu of foreclosure.

THE LESSON:

◆   *Taking time to contact the debtor and asking if he or she would like me to buy their loan totally changes the relationship and dynamics.*

ENTREPRENEURIAL
REFLECTIONS

20

DON'T DISMISS
WHAT'S JUST NEXT DOOR

My friend and fellow bank director Jim owned a company that sold uninterrupted power supplies and surge protectors. His company was growing and he needed a larger building. Jim called me one day to ask that I evaluate a building he was seriously considering purchasing. Unfortunately, three other real estate agents were already involved in the deal, so as a real estate agent, I concluded that there was no more room for a commission for me in this transaction. But, I still agreed to evaluate his prospective new location. As I always do when looking at real estate, I also looked at the surrounding properties as well as the one I had been requested to tour. The building next door was so similar to the desired property that I went in to look around. After proceeding through most of this occupied location, I was intercepted by the office manager. His mission was to quickly and politely throw me out. As he was leading me to the front door, we passed what was obviously the boss's office. I detoured into that office. The manager, not realizing that I was no longer following him, continued on without me. I quickly introduced myself to the boss, and by the time the manager realized I wasn't following him and returned to retrieve me, the boss waved him off and we continued our friendly conversation.

The boss told me that he owned both the business and the building. I explained that my friend was looking for a building like his and was considering the building next to his. I would appreciate any insight he might offer about the building and the area. The boss explained that he had actually been considering selling his building, but he had not put it on the market because he hadn't quite determined how to deal with a foundation problem. By the time I left, I knew what the foundation problem was and what the boss wanted for his building. I then went by Jim's office and suggested that he look at this building before closing on the next door property. Jim looked at the building, felt it was ideal for his company, and having an engineering background, believed the foundation problem was not nearly as serious as the price discount it generated. Jim bought the building, and I received all the commission on the full $500,000 purchase price.

A similar situation occurred with respect to a property I owned and wanted to sell. As discussed in the previous chapter, this was one of the two properties I had received in lieu of foreclosure. Because I had worked with this debtor in good faith as I had with all of them, when he was unable to pay his note, he gave me the deed on a vacant lakeside lot at Lake Kiowa, Texas, a small gated community a few miles south of the Oklahoma-Texas border. By telephone, I engaged a real estate agent whose office was located just outside the gates of Lake Kiowa to list my property and hopefully identify its ultimate buyer. After 6-8 weeks of no activity, on a Saturday morning I decided to drive up and look at this property I now owned. After convincing the guard at the front gate that I was a property owner, he gave me access and pointed me in the general direction of my lot. When I arrived, there was nothing much to see. It looked like all the other lake front lots. I did notice the next door neighbor was mowing his lawn. When I approached him, he cut off the mower to talk. I told him that I now owned the lot next door, didn't know anything about local real estate values, and asked him what he thought my lake lot property was worth. He was reluctant to give me a price, and I finally asked, "How much would you pay believing you were buying it way below market?" With that, he gave me a price, and I simply said, "Sold." He offered to get his checkbook to write an earnest money check. I suggested that he wait until Monday morning and drop by the real estate agent's office to work up a contract. So, I sold my property to my next door neighbor in all of 15 minutes, and my real estate agent received a not-so-deserved full commission on the sale.

These two sales illustrate a fundamental principle of mine regarding real estate transactions: Never casually dismiss the owners of adjacent property. In many cases, they are the world's leading experts on the property you're looking at. This principle frequently applies to non-real estate ventures as well. Often people standing quietly on the sidelines can provide valuable information.

THE LESSONS:

◆   *Never casually dismiss the owners of adjacent properties.*

◆   *Often people standing quietly on the sidelines can provide valuable information.*

21
KNOW WHAT
YOU'RE WORTH

O ver the years, I've been the principal player in numerous entrepreneurial companies that in total have employed thousands of people. In all of these companies, we've made it clear that if any employee was capable of handling a better job than we could provide, we would help him or her get it outside of our company. In keeping with that philosophy and commitment, Mark was a young man who had originally been a counselor in our summer youth ranch program, then was promoted and had been an equally outstanding youth ranch program director the summer prior to and following graduating from college. When the summer ended, he wanted to stay on at the ranch, but we didn't have an opening deserving of his capabilities. For his benefit, I insisted that he focus on advancing his career. A few days later, I was invited by a neighbor to a party and was introduced to a friend of theirs visiting from Tennessee. The friend, Mr. Rhett Ball, was a fine southern gentlemen and the President/CEO of American Health Profiles. At that time, the company provided mobile multi-phase health testing to the members of various unions. I arranged for him to meet and interview Mark. Mark was immediately offered a job and shortly thereafter moved to Tennessee to join American Health Profiles.

A few months later, I decided to take a year off and leased the ranch. I had stayed in touch with Mark, and he shared with Mr. Ball my intention to take a sabbatical. Mr. Ball picked up the phone and in his soft-talking southern style, convinced me to fly to Nashville and discuss a project they were about to begin. When I arrived, he told me they were in the final stages of discussions with the world's largest agriculture co-op, Farmland Industries, to provide mobile multi-phase health testing to the rural community members of their nearly 2,000 local co-ops located throughout the Midwest. He knew from our original meeting that I had rural Midwest agricultural background and wanted me to head up opening this new market. The fact that I was trying to avoid work, not find it, and was used to being my own boss put me in a very strong position when we did negotiate my joining the project. As the great negotiator Herb Cohen always preached when negotiating, "Care, but not too much." I finally agreed to come aboard for six months to launch the project.

At that point, Mr. Ball asked me what I thought I should receive in compensation. Aware that the company had in excess of 100 employees, I told him that neither he nor I had any idea what I was worth in that position. However, if I were to join the effort, I had two requirements: first, understanding that the company founder and Mr. Ball would obviously both be better paid than me, I wanted to be the third best paid person in the company and initially didn't care if it was only by $1. I felt that if they weren't willing to bring me in at that level, I was not interested in postponing my sabbatical to be part of the project. Second, after 90 days, I wanted to sit down with Mr. Ball. At that time, with a little experience behind us, we could decide what I was worth.

Rhett agreed. Ninety days later we were at Farmland Industries' headquarters in Kansas City staying at the then-newly-opened Crown Center. Mr. Ball invited me to his suite and, reminding me that my 90 days was up, wanted to know what I now felt I was worth. I told him that I had written the exact dollar figure on a piece of paper that was in my shirt pocket, but I added that I felt that it was much more important to know what he felt I was worth. His offer was a mammoth increase. At that point, I removed and unfolded the paper in my pocket. It was identical to the offer he had just made.

That soft-talking southern gentleman managed to keep me on-board for almost two years. It was the only salaried job I ever held after leaving Kodak, but it was a fascinating and rewarding experience. I was offered Mr. Ball's job when he announced that he was going to retire. I had, however, already stayed longer than planned and was overdue to re-enter my own entrepreneurial world.

The biggest bonus from my time with American Health Profiles was meeting their vice-president, Bettye Akin, and we married eight years later. Another plus was that Mr. Ball convinced me to attend Harvard's OPM entrepreneurial program. The program is a total of nine weeks, three weeks each year for three years. The experience enhanced and expanded my business and personal lives in many wonderful ways. I highly recommend it.

THE LESSONS:

◆ *Dollars are only a small part of compensation.*

◆ *Agreeing to reevaluate your offer after you've proven yourself is more important than your opening salary.*

22

WE'RE NOT
TALKING ABOUT "NEED"

Statistical organizations like Standard & Poor's who track business divide business into numerous categories. One of those categories is Consumer – Discretionary. Early in my business career, I encountered a small 100 year-old company that made "hand-made, made-to-measure" custom cowboy boots. The company produced magnificent work and could turn out ten to twelve pairs of boots a day but wasn't getting enough orders to keep them busy. I believed that the company should be overrun with orders and I set out to prove it. Having just wrapped up a major project, I was ready to take on a project that had having fun as its #1 goal. The boot venture struck me as the perfect venue.

I engaged a travel trailer manufacturer to customize one of their small trailers. The door to the back 1/3 of the trailer opened to an aisle with shelving on both sides. These shelves were filled with sample boots. The front of the trailer was a small but well-appointed, comfortable living room/showroom.

I enticed a very bright and personable young lady, Katie Barclay, who had worked for me at American Health Profiles to sign on for the venture. While I oversaw the customizing of the trailer and developed our marketing plan, Katie spent several weeks at the bootmaker's shop learning how to measure to ensure properly fitting boots and learning the construction details and the benefits of our product.

With everything ready and full of enthusiasm, we loaded up, hitched up, and headed out of the DFW Metroplex for West Texas. We went to small ranch communities like Dimmit, Muleshoe, and Hereford. Between getting acquainted with the local motel manager/ owner, locating the local café where the ranchers met for coffee/ breakfast, and using reciprocity privileges at local country clubs, within 36 hours we could identify most of the top prospects in the county for high-dollar handmade, made-to-measure boots.

We were a bit of a novelty (a dog and pony show come to town), and the word spread quickly. Additionally, we had a very long phone cord that we connected in one of our motel rooms and ran out to the trailer so we could make calls while waiting for appointments or drop-ins. We were definitely pre-cell phone.

Enough interesting happenings took place on this adventure to fill this book. However, a few stand out in my memory:

Katie was measuring the President of a small-town bank southwest of Amarillo, and he and I were talking about the local economy. There were a lot of feedlots in the area, and locals still talked about the cattle market taking a dive a few years earlier (they called it "the wreck.") When the subject came up, the banker looked at me and deadly serious, said, "Jay, I never knew I was a millionaire until I lost over a million dollars in the wreck and was able to avoid taking bankruptcy."

The fact that we were operating in the consumer – discretionary market was made clear to me one day when I overheard Katie's discussion with a prospective customer. This West Texas rancher said, "Little lady, I don't need no cowboy boots. I have 36 pair of cowboy boots."

Katie responded, "Sir, we're not discussing 'need.'" She sold him a pair of white ostrich boots.

While we were back in the Dallas-Fort Worth area celebrating a highly successful West Texas trip, we met a man who sold high-end custom made suits to top executives in Dallas-Ft. Worth, Oklahoma City, and Tulsa. He took his samples to their offices, measured them and wrote up their orders at their place of work. We quickly put a referral agreement in place and overnight we started calling on oilmen, bankers, lawyers, doctors, and corporate executives at their offices. Because of his referrals, our first trip to Tulsa was unbelievably successful.

In those days many of the top Country & Western stars were represented by an agency located, not in Nashville as one might expect, but in Tulsa, Oklahoma. I sent our newly hired second salesman up to call on them, and Katie went along to observe our new man in action. Larry played things close to the vest and, had Katie not gone along, I never would have heard this story. In one day working the agents, Larry sold each of them at least one pair of boots and some bought two and three pairs.

Only the agency owner had not ordered or shown any interest. Near day's end, Larry walked into the owner's palatial office unannounced and said, "Sir, I have to know! Why haven't you ordered a single pair of our fine boots?"

The boss looked up from behind his massive walnut desk and replied, "I bought a pair of custom-made high dollar boots a few years ago, and they leaked."

Larry opened his sample case, pulled out the highest dollar sample he had, walked over to the boss's wet bar, filled the boot with water, walked back and set it on the man's fancy desk. Larry then engaged him in a sports conversation they had started in the coffee room earlier. The man visited but never took his eyes off of the boot. About fifteen minutes later, Larry picked up the boot, returned to the wet bar, and poured the water down the drain. With that, he said, "If you will slip off your shoes, Katie can measure you while we select the leather and design your boots. I would recommend Ostrich for your first pair. Which of these colors do you prefer?"

At one point we were lost on a back road and flagged down a mud covered pickup driven by a man I figured for a ranch hand. He was so accommodating that I suggested he come by our trailer for coffee when he was in town. He did and bought one pair of the least expensive (never say cheapest) boots we sold.

While our new friend the ranch hand, Carl Brugal, was being measured, he asked if we had ever taken our boot trailer to Amarillo, TX, about 45 miles northeast of Hereford, TX where we were located that morning. I said, "No," and I explained that while we were good at quickly getting acquainted and identifying prospects in the small communities, Amarillo was just too big of a market for us to tackle.

Carl said he had to be in Amarillo later in the week and would meet us and make some introductions. Since he had purchased the least expensive pair of boots we sold and Amarillo was so big, I wasn't much impressed with our chances of selling many boots. However, from day one, we had placed a priority on having fun in the boot business, and Carl was an enjoyable fellow. Carl said he had a meeting at his bank on Thursday that would be over about 10:00, so we agreed to meet him at the bank then. We arrived a few minutes early and, while sitting in the lobby, I picked up the bank quarterly financial statement that was lying on the coffee table.

I about fell out of my chair when I read it and learned that it was indeed Carl's bank. He owned the bank.

While I was recovering my composure, Carl showed up. When he introduced us to the bank president, Bo, it became old-home week. Bo and I had sat next to each other on an American Airline's flight a few weeks earlier and had enjoyed a pleasant conversation.

While the four of us were visiting, I mentioned that I had always wanted to meet Amarillo Slim, the famous poker player and one of the early winners of the Vegas Million Dollar Poker Tournament.

During the week we were in Amarillo, Carl and Bo sent us a constant stream of boot buyers, many of whom had never owned a pair.

On our second morning, there was a knock on the trailer door and, when I opened it, there stood Amarillo Slim. (Allow me to add that he did not look happy about being there). Fortunately, Katie was a looker and a charmer, and Slim got hooked. He came back for coffee and to chat every morning until we left Amarillo.

The morning before we left town, he arrived considerably later than usual, and I asked him why he was late. Slim explained that he had been at the jail and had just left Cullen Davis's jail cell. Besides the weather, the hottest thing in Amarillo while we were there was the murder trial of T. Cullen Davis, a Fort Worth millionaire who was accused of murdering Stan Farr, the lover of Cullen's estranged wife Priscilla, at the Davis mansion in Fort Worth. Cullen's prominence in Fort Worth had caused the prosecution to be granted a change in venue for the murder trial, and Amarillo had been agreed upon as the location. That summer, Amarillo became the closest thing to a media circus Texas had seen in a long time.

The murder trial was of more than a passing interest to me. Stan's sister Linda (Texas Lil) had been a friendly competitor of my corporate dude ranch Ranchland, and Linda had been devastated by the loss of her brother. How or if Amarillo Slim and Cullen Davis were previously acquainted, I don't know, but I was curious about the reaction of Amarillo Slim, a great student of people, as are all great poker players. When I asked about his time at the jail with Cullen Davis, Amarillo Slim said, "I have a $20,000 bet that he will walk away from the trial a free man. I am totally comfortable with my bet, but I have never looked into the eyes of a guiltier son-of-a-bitch in my life."

Davis was ultimately acquitted, a tribute to the fine lawyering of Houston's Richard "Racehorse" Haynes. The case was perhaps a precursor to the much more famous case involving O.J. Simpson. It's not hard to predict what the now-deceased Amarillo Slim would have said about that one. But, I've never forgotten the importance of studying people.

THE LESSONS:

◆ *Selling a product or business doesn't have to be about addressing needs. People make decisions based on desire. Sell to what people want, and you'll always win.*

◆ *Make sure your business includes having fun.*

ENTREPRENEURIAL
REFLECTIONS

23

IS YOUR WORD
YOUR BOND?

S ilver, like most commodities, fluctuates in value over time. At no time in my life did silver fluctuate more in value than in the early 1980s. The best-known reason for the fluctuation in value then was the attempt by Herbert, Bunker and Lamar Hunt to corner the silver market. Sons of famed oil wildcatter H.L. Hunt and billionaires themselves individually, the Hunt brothers knew quite a lot about commodities. The more silver they acquired and controlled, the higher the price of silver went. My work with photo finishers and x-ray film at Kodak had made me very knowledgeable regarding recovering silver from film and photo processing.

It was in this environment that I was dedicating time to acquiring and reselling silver-laden x-ray film.

I had an opportunity to buy several thousand pounds of silver-laden x-ray film from a Nashville firm. Before going to Nashville to take delivery, I made some calls, located a refinery in the hills of Tennessee about 60 miles out of Nashville and made a firm deal to sell him the film. The price we agreed on would, after all my expenses, give me a net profit of about $20,000. Because of the activities of the Hunt Brothers, the price of silver had increased substantially by the time I arrived in Nashville. I pointed this fact out to my buyer and demanded a higher price than we had agreed on. He rightly refused, and my greed left me without a buyer. I spent the next several days in Nashville trying to sell the silver-laden x-ray film which I was paying a security firm to guard. In the process, I ran up a $600 phone bill and a significant hotel bill. On the 4th day, the price of silver had moved up a little more but was becoming a bit erratic. At that point, I admitted to myself that, in trying to re-trade the deal, I had abandoned my ethics and been a greedy jerk. With that self-confession behind me, I did the only smart thing I had done in the entire process. I swallowed my pride, called my original buyer, admitted to having been out of line, and offered to honor our original agreement. My buyer refused but countered with an offer a little less than we had originally agreed upon. I replied, "I had that coming; I accept."

I was paid and delivered the silver-laden film early in the afternoon on March 27, 1980, the day known as Silver Thursday.

Before the commodity markets closed that afternoon, silver crashed, falling to $10.80. Before the crash, silver had reached an all-time high of $49.45. Had the sale not been completed before the crash, my net worth would have suffered a major blow. Additionally, I would have been left owing the bank the $100,000 I had borrowed to finance the purchase.

As I flew home, I promised myself that, going forward, my word and my business ethics would always be more important than profit.

A couple of sidelines to my story of silver and greed: When I arrived in Nashville to purchase the x-ray film, after examining the film, I called my bank to fund the loan I had arranged. As it happened, Walter was out of the bank when I called, so I left the instructions with his secretary to have him fund the x-ray film loan. By the time Walter got back to the bank, every young lady in the bank had been told, "That Jay Rodgers is over in Tennessee buying X-Rated films."

When I made the deal to purchase the x-ray film, I was smoking four packs of Camels a day. By the end of the third day in Nashville, I was up to five packs a day. At this point, I had not thought of calling, let alone mustered up the courage to call, the original refinery back and panic was setting in. That night I told God that if he would get me out of this mess, I would go home and quit smoking. Yeah, like I was doing him a favor. Deserved or not, He gave me a double win. I survived financially, and, at 76, I'm alive and in good health. I smoked my last cigarette on April 4, 1980.

THE LESSON:

◆ *Build a legacy and a business based on integrity.*
Do what you say, and say what you mean. In
the business world, unfortunately, lawyers have
replaced handshakes. I believe the very best
contract is one that clearly and simply expresses all
parties' intents, is signed, and then put in a filing
cabinet never to be retrieved.

ENTREPRENEURIAL
REFLECTIONS

24
HAVE A PLAN

Three years after my wife Bettye and I formed our healthcare staffing company, we set the date for selling the company an additional three years out, and circled it on the calendar, June 30, 1990. I believed that having audited financial statements would be a great advantage in selling our company, so over three years before our targeted sales date I engaged Deloitte, Haskins & Sells to annually audit the books of our company. I have never been completely convinced that professional fees bear much relationship to the time actually spent even though attorneys and CPAs all purport to and may well bill by the hour. Because I thought that Deloitte would charge more and more each year as they saw that I was growing and getting closer and closer to selling the company, I insisted on a three-year bid for the three years of audited financials I would need before our anticipated sale. I told them we would grow at least 400% over the next three years. Deloitte initially resisted but finally relented and gave me the three-year quote I had asked for.

We missed our targeted sale date by 45 days. However, because we sold to a public company, the buyer insisted that we engage Deloitte to provide an audit opinion covering the last 45 days we owned the business. Deloitte's bill to us for the 45 day stub period exceeded the entire amount we paid them for the preceding fiscal year. Upon receipt of Deloitte's bill, I could only laugh.

THE LESSONS:

◆ *Draw your own conclusions and plan and negotiate accordingly.*

◆ *Be specific with your plan. Many brilliant entrepreneurs have failed without a clear plan. It's awfully hard to get there if you don't know where you're going.*

25

AVOID DANGEROUS
CONCENTRATIONS

Many readers will be acquainted with the danger of a small business having one or two customers that represent a significant portion of their revenues and/or profits. Some might pick a slightly higher or lower number, or the nature of the business might encourage a higher or lower number. My rule of thumb is: No customer should represent over 15% of your revenues. The danger is that if the customer goes away, much of the fixed overhead that you have taken on to serve that customer will not go away. Bankers are particularly wary of lending to a customer with this problem.

My wife Bettye, Robert Fielder (a long-time employee, then partner), and I formed Healthcare Staff Resources with $3,000 in capital. The mission of HSR was to provide physical therapists, occupational therapists, and pharmacists to healthcare facilities. In North Texas, there is perhaps no bigger health care provider than Parkland Hospital. As Dallas County's public hospital, Parkland sees more patients each year than any of its privately owned competitors. We at HSR were therefore overjoyed when Parkland contracted with us to provide Physical Therapists and Occupational Therapists to Parkland. HSR began to grow rapidly as Parkland ordered more and more coverage. At a monthly board meeting, I learned that almost over-night Parkland had become our largest customer and accounted for over 40% of our revenue. As chairman, I was able to get agreement on and institute a policy that forbade the company from allowing a customer to represent over 15% of our revenues. Additionally, we agreed that even at the risk of losing the Parkland account, within 45 days we would be in compliance with our new policy. We were still small enough and growing fast enough that these policies would not inflict a mortal wound.

We did lose the Parkland account. I'm happy to report, however, that less than 60 days after we lost it, Parkland announced that they would no longer be working with outside OT and PT staffing firms and that all funds for this staffing had been cut off.

As I mentioned earlier, having too much revenue concentrated among one or two customers is dangerous. Equally dangerous but less commonly discussed is the danger of a small business having only one source of supply for any unique or critical item. When we started Smart Start, we knew on day one that, to build a meaningful business and control our own destiny, we would have to have our own ignition interlock device. The fact is that it took a great deal longer than we originally anticipated, but we were able to build our own device and had an outside firm manufacture per our specifications.

As chairman for over a year, I encouraged the CEO to seek a

second source for the manufacture of our device. At that point, I gave him a very-easy-to-understand ultimatum regarding a second source for our device. Five months later, the second source was producing a few devices for us. Thirty days after that, totally unaware that we even had a second source, our original manufacturer informed us that they were restructuring their company and product line effective immediately and would no longer be able to supply us. It had taken almost 6 months to get our second source up to speed, but they were able to take over without causing a supply problem. Six months without units would have been disastrous to our growing business. Needless to say, we immediately set about establishing another second source.

THE LESSON:

◆ *As you build your business, make sure that you, not a supplier or a customer, are in charge and control your destiny.*

ENTREPRENEURIAL
REFLECTIONS

26

BE WILLING TO
ADMIT YOUR MISTAKES
AND DO WHAT IT TAKES

I have always believed that when you have a problem in business, the quicker you face up to it and address it, the better off you are. Ideally, you will contact your affected customers before the problem and consequences come to their attention. Explain the problem. Take responsibility for the problem. Explain to them the plan you have put in place to correct the issue. Give them a timetable for solving the issue and take whatever steps are necessary to retain them as loyal customers.

Unfortunately, in some cases, you aren't made aware of the problem until it's too late to follow the course of action outlined above. Such was the case with a mistake we made some twenty-eight years ago when we were in the business of staffing healthcare professionals. At this stage in my life, I can look back on the incident and laugh. However, let me assure you that it wasn't funny at the time.

A large hospital located just a few miles from our offices retained us to identify and recruit a new director for their pharmacy. We found the perfect individual. The hospital administrator was ecstatic and hired the man with the agreement that he would start in forty-five days. With our task accomplished, our billing department sent the hospital an invoice for the agreed upon fee of $25,000.

Two days later while we were sitting around patting ourselves on the back for a job well done, I received a call from the hospital administrator. The words "livid" and "irate" grossly understate the administrator's frame of mind when I answered his call.

The administrator, as it turned out, had not yet informed his current pharmacy director that he was being replaced. He had planned to wait until the date for his new hire's arrival was closer. Unfortunately, our billing department had made it a moot issue. Rather than sending our invoice directly to the hospital administrator, they sent it to the hospital's pharmacy director. The pharmacy director, seeing the invoice and realizing that he was being replaced, had just walked into the administrator's office with our invoice in hand and asked the administrator if there was something he needed to know.

Needless to say, it was not our finest hour. When you make a mistake, handle it, and move on.

Because we provided staffing services to hospitals and other healthcare providers, many assumed that a lengthy collections cycle was the inevitable result of the business niche we had chosen to enter. I was unwilling to accept that assessment. When our A/R aging got totally out of hand, I announced at a company meeting that we would reduce our collections cycle to 20 days for all privately owned healthcare facilities we served and 45 days for all government facilities. Helen, our CFO, promptly announced that this goal could not be achieved. My response: "We're going to do it, and we're sure going to miss you." I promptly assigned collections as the #1 priority of one of our employees.

A good collections person must be temperamentally suited to the task. The task requires persistence, a thick skin, a pleasant demeanor and the assertiveness to politely call the customer to account when it turns out that the check really wasn't in the mail. Our collections cycle was reduced to less than 20 days (18 to be precise) for our privately owned customer and to 45 days for our government accounts. Although it's incorrect to assert that nothing is impossible, most things are possible. We don't ever know what's actually possible until we fully commit to achieving the goal. You have to do what it takes until it works. That was the approach we used with our clients. Although we were the world's best medical staffing company, we were totally inept in the banking world.

The value of proper policies and procedures was proven again when we sold Healthcare Staffing Resources to Kimberly Quality Care, a division of the NYSE exchange company Lifetime. Their President, Larry Stusser, was concerned that we had receivables of nearly $500,000 on the books and had only a $5,000 allowance for bad debt. Rather than rewrite the definitive agreement, we resolved the issue by shaking hands on a gentlemen's agreement that, 120 days after the closing, I would send Larry a check for all receivables on the books at closing exceeding $5,000 that had not been collected. In turn, he would send me a check for any of the $5,000 that had not been needed to cover uncollected receivables on the books at closing. Fewer than 90 days after the closing, I received his check in the amount of $5,000.

Incidentally, Helen got on board with our collections goal, remained as the company's CFO, and performed admirably all the way through our selling of the company. In addition to her company bonus at sale, I rewarded her with 5,000 shares of stock in our next venture which I started two years later. The company recently sold, and her 5,000 shares got her a million dollar check.

Despite the fact that "It can be done"…if you believe it can't, you'll be right.

THE LESSON:

◆ *Mistakes are a part of life. Admit them, address them, and move on.*

27

UNDERSTAND YOUR PROSPECT'S MOTIVATIONS

In the process of selling our healthcare staffing business, I spent significant time identifying prospective buyers for our company. One of those prospects, Hooper Holmes, initially stood out from the rest. I succeeded in securing an audience with a decision-maker, and a visit was arranged for an executive of the company to evaluate our business and report on how suitable our company was for acquisition by Hooper Holmes.

I spent my time telling her what a great, clean, well-run company we were selling. I showed her our business in detail, including our financial statements, introductions to key operating personnel, and references from well-known customers. She listened and observed intently. Our company was a perfect addition to their core business.

Upon her departure, I was convinced that I had landed our buyer. I was surprised a few days later to receive a communication that Hooper Holmes would not be proceeding with the acquisition of our business. Believing that Hooper had been the perfect prospect, even though the opportunity had been lost, I did some digging – due diligence I should have done prior to her arrival, not after. It turned out that the VP who had visited to assess our business had originally been an RN in a management position with Hooper Holmes. A few years earlier, she had brought an acquisition opportunity to the company's attention. They acquired the company and, because it was in her area of expertise, put her in charge of that acquisition. In only two years, she had doubled revenues, tripled profits, and was rewarded with a promotion to VP and a major raise.

This information was readily available; in fact, she had mentioned the prior acquisition while she was there touring my company. If I had listened to her as carefully as she had listened to me, I would have realized that she was interested in buying a business that offered an opportunity for her to shine. She was looking for a repeat of her earlier success. I had convinced her that we had a smooth, well-run business with little room for improvement. Had I done my homework and understood her perspective, I would have spent my time talking about the opportunities we had not bothered to pursue and the mistakes we had made. My presentation had, unfortunately, been very effective. I convinced her that our company offered her little opportunity for another overnight success story.

To this day, I believe Hooper Holmes should have bought our company, but I've never forgotten the painful lesson I learned. I now do my due diligence before, not after, the presentation. I focus on what the buyer wants to buy, not what I am trying to sell. That means I ask a lot of questions, listen closely to the answers, and put my ego and pride aside.

THE LESSON:

◆ *Do your research and understand what motivates someone.*

ENTREPRENEURIAL REFLECTIONS

28
THERE ARE
NO CRYSTAL BALLS

When Bettye and I were in the process of selling our healthcare staffing company, my M & A attorney, David Hammer, and I traveled to Boston to negotiate with buyer Kimberly Quality Care and its counsel.

When we arrived at the buyer's offices in Boston and were ushered into the conference room, a team of three, including their legal counsel, were already seated and awaiting our arrival. They had a prepared agenda that listed all the issues that needed to be resolved.

The President of Kimberly Quality Care, the decision maker, was, however, not at the table. When I asked where he was, the team explained that he had been delayed but would be joining us later. I replied that his delay was fortunate as I had always wanted to explore downtown Boston. With that, I told the buyer's team to call my cell phone when the President arrived and I would return. As I left, I assured them that they could accomplish a great deal working with my M & A attorney until their President arrived and

I returned. Remember, NEVER, NEVER, NEVER allow yourself
to get into a negotiation where your side is the only side that can
make a final decision or commitment.

While our preference was for an all-cash deal, the buyer had
proposed using its publicly traded shares as a small part of the consideration for the purchase. We had researched the stock of parent
company Lifetime Corporation (NYSE) and had found its pricing to
be highly stable, hovering at around $35 per share and with a long-
term uptrend. When the buyer repeated its desire to use its stock as
partial consideration, I countered with the position that we would
accept provided that the shares were registered and therefore freely
transferable at issuance. In the days before shelf registrations enabled
public companies to issue registered shares at a moment's notice, my
request was met with the comment that it would take some weeks
to register and deliver those shares to us. My response: Provide for
additional cash compensation equal to the reduction in value if the
share price declines between closing and the delivery of registered
tradeable shares to us.

David advised that I was jeopardizing the transaction over an
issue of little impact given the stability of the shares. When the
meeting ended, both sides instructed our respective counsel to continue to work on the definitive agreement pending resolution of this
remaining issue. The buyer ultimately relented, and counsel included
a provision that, if the value of the shares declined before they were
registered and tradeable, I would receive additional compensation in
the amount of the loss in market value of my shares.

We closed on this multimillion dollar transaction on August 10,

1990. Before the stock was tradeable, the US initiated Desert Storm and the stock market dropped precipitously. The additional dollars we received definitely had more than "a little impact" on the deal. The price per share later returned to its pre-invasion level. We materially enhanced the value of the transaction to our shareholders solely because I refused to accept the past and the present as the predictor of the future.

THE LESSON:

◆ *Don't predict. Protect.*

ENTREPRENEURIAL
REFLECTIONS

"ENTREPRENEURS AND THEIR

SMALL ENTERPRISES ARE RESPONSIBLE

FOR ALMOST ALL THE ECONOMIC GROWTH

IN THE UNITED STATES."

RONALD REAGAN

29

MY MOST
SUCCESSFUL FAILURE

I f you've ever failed, as most of us have, you've learned quite a
few lessons.

While attending Harvard's Owner/President Management Program in the early 90s, I developed what has proven to be a life-long
close friendship with Ruth Freiman, a fellow classmate who resided
in Ottawa, Canada. Over lunch one day, I casually mentioned that I
had always wanted to attend the Calgary Stampede. Having briefly rodeoed and ridden saddle broncos and bareback horses in my
younger days (however not very successfully), I was well aware
that it was considered the world's best rodeo. Ruth responded,
"Then why the heck don't you?" She went on to mention that she
and her husband were good friends of Bill Pratt, who had been the
General Manager of the rodeo for many years. Ruth contacted Bill
and the result was that in 1999, Bill arranged for Bettye and me
to be invited as VIP guests of the Calgary Stampede. The die was
cast, and this past summer was our 17th consecutive summer trip to
Calgary. Bettye and I quickly got into the habit of arriving a couple

of weeks before the Stampede and making up for that by staying
a couple of weeks after it ended. We even bought a condo for use
during our summer visits.

Over the years, Bettye and I developed relationships with the officers and directors of the Stampede, and these friendships became the
primary reason we continue to spend summers there. The Stampede
is quite a spectacle, and one of the most exciting events is the Chuck
Wagon Races. I call the event "The NASCAR of the North," 36
drivers, 4 horse teams and chuck wagons participate in heats of four
(nine races each of the ten nights). In addition to the nightly prize,
the top winner for the ten performances receives $100,000. Because
corporations compete to sponsor the chuck wagons, the Stampede
created an auction whereby prospective sponsors could bid for the
right to provide the chuck wagon tarp complete with the corporate
logo for their driver. It's not unusual for the winning bid for the best
driver's wagon to top $150,000. The Stampede divides the take be-
tween the driver and the Stampede.

After noting many similarities and common interests between
my friends in Calgary and my friends in Texas (energy and ranching being two of the biggest),I decided that next year I would put
together a consortium of Texas sponsors for a chuck wagon with
a tarp styled "Texas Friends of the Calgary Stampede." The tarp
would feature a different sponsoring Texas company each of the ten
nights. I didn't consider the challenge of raising $200,000 for the
auction and funding ten nights of social events at the Wagon Barn
to be difficult. Many of the companies I had decided to approach
were Texas-based companies already doing a lot of business in
Calgary. I personally put up a $10,000 deposit with Jason Glass, a

past champion driver in the chuck wagon races. When I returned
to Texas after that summer, I resolved to get introduced into the
Houston oil & gas community which I felt represented the biggest
pool of my prospective Texas sponsors.

I called Houston attorney friend Gary Trichter and scheduled a
meeting. At the last minute, Gary was called out of town but recruit-
ed his friend Carolyn Faulk to meet with us. Carolyn is the successful owner and operator of a Houston-based plastics distribution
business and is also a director of the Houston rodeo. Carolyn listened
attentively to my plan and invited us to dinner that evening to discuss
it further. Because it was Bettye's and my anniversary, I declined by
telling Carolyn that we already had anniversary reservations at Café
Annie's, an exclusive Houston restaurant now known as "RDG."
After Bettye and I had been seated there that evening, the waiter
delivered a bottle of Dom Perignon to the table and announced that
it was courtesy of Carolyn. When it came time for us to leave and
I asked for the check, the waiter announced that the check had also
been taken care of courtesy of Carolyn. An incredibly gracious ges-
ture by someone we had just met.

Over time, Carolyn introduced us to numerous directors of the
Houston Rodeo and to many of its officers. They in turn introduced
us to executives at several of the Texas companies doing business in
Calgary which I had targeted as potential sponsors of our chuck wagon. I had gone so far as to engage an artist to do a colorful contempo-
rary painting of a racing chuck wagon.

TEXAS Friends of the CALGARY STAMPEDE

I used the artwork both in my presentations to the sponsors and on t-shirts. Unfortunately, my best efforts to enlist sponsors and raise the funds were less than successful. I only received pledges for about half of the funds needed and ended up releasing those. Although less than successful is kinder and gentler, the fact is that my efforts failed. I threw in the towel when I finally realized that I had not properly analyzed the project. The lesson I learned was that Texas companies doing business in Calgary wanted to pass themselves off as companies with roots in the Calgary community and did not want to attract attention as interlopers. They worked hard to fly under the radar and be successful while maintaining a low profile.

When forced to acknowledge my failure, I engaged an artist to paint a picture in morbid colors of a chuck wagon being driven over a cliff. I presented both artist renderings the next summer at a Calgary party we hosted for our friends there and where I was compelled to concede defeat. That painting still hangs in my office to remind me of the experience and the lessons I learned.

But all was not lost. My newfound friends at the Houston Rodeo invited me to participate with the Valley Lodge Trail Riders Association that rides into Houston each year to open the Houston Rodeo. My participation led to an invitation to be a guest of the board for the annual week-long ride in south Texas with the Tejas Vaqueros, a great group of 350 horsemen of which I am now a full-fledged member. Other contacts arranged for me to ride as a guest of the board with the 1,000 member riding group near Santa Barbara, California, Los Rancheros Visitadores, a great organization of which Ronald Reagan was a member. Carolyn Faulk and a couple of her friends have joined a group that Bettye and I cruise with annually, and they are outstanding additions to our crowd.

As expressed in the chapter title, the chuck wagon tarp experience was definitely one of my most successful and rewarding failures.

THE LESSON:

- ◆ *Always look for the gems that hide in the rubble.*

30
HARVARD TAKEAWAYS

One of the great learning experiences of my life was when I enrolled in the Harvard Business School's Owner/President Management Program (OPM). The Harvard Business School invites business owners from all over the world to attend the nine week program; it is held three-weeks each year for three consecutive years. In the early 1990s, the cost was $10,000 per year for each of the three years. I now understand that the yearly cost exceeds $30,000.

While the Harvard professors were good, I believe that I learned more from the other entrepreneurs in attendance than the faculty. However, here are two specifics I did learn from Harvard professor Paul Vatter that proved to be worth far more than the cost of the entire three years. The first was the concept of BATNA. BATNA is an acronym, standing for "Best Alternative to a Negotiated Agreement."

I have always had a great deal of confidence in my negotiating skills, but those skills are of limited use when the other party is unwilling to negotiate when their BATNA is to do nothing. That was the dilemma facing my friend Norm. Norm is an enormously wealthy, accomplished individual, the holder of 40+ U.S. patents and the builder of highly successful concrete and plastics businesses now operated by his two sons Peter and Jon. One of Norm's many interests is aviation. He developed and received FAA approval for an $800,000 modification on the Piper Malibu airplane. Norm immediately recognized the value of what he had created but had little time to exploit it commercially. Instead, he identified three partners that had the facilities, tools, and expertise to modify the planes. The four of them formed a company to exploit the technology. Norm's partners were in fact successful, but they were far from grateful. They were collectively in control of the recently formed company. They used their control to not pay dividends, to overpay themselves, and to sub work to a company they owned apart from Norm. Exasperated, Norm asked to be bought out. His partners offered only a small fraction of what Norm's interest was worth.

When Norm called me to complain about the treachery of his partners, I remembered the Harvard lesson on BATNA. I began to think about ways to compel the threesome to deal fairly with my friend. Rather than focusing on Norm's BATNA, I decided to change their BATNA which was to (1.) overpay themselves, (2.) sub work to their other company, and (3.) pay no dividends. Norm had formed Wallingford Associates LLC specifically to hold his equity in the venture, and he gave me complete control of Wallingford Associates. I immediately wrote a nice letter to the terrible trio telling them that as the new CEO and President of Wallingford, I was looking forward to working with them. The response was exactly as I had anticipated. I received absolutely no response from any of my three Fed-Exed letters. Thirty days later, having done my homework, I sent a second letter explaining that because of their paltry offer to buy Norm out and their unwillingness to communicate with me, I had been in touch with a major non-profit that was exceptionally well-versed on minority positions and that giving them all or part of Norm's ownership of Wallingford Associates would be much more financially rewarding to Norm than accepting their offer. In keeping with my conviction that the best bluff is no bluff at all, I attached the following letter.

NATIONAL ASSOCIATION FOR THE ADVANCEMENT OF COLORED PEOPLE
4805 MT. HOPE DRIVE • BALTIMORE, MD 21215-3297 • (410) 358-8900

KWEISI MFUME
President & Chief Executive Officer

OFFICE OF THE GENERAL COUNSEL

JULIAN BOND
Chairman, Board of Directors

January 16, 2003

VIA FACSIMILE & REGULAR MAIL

Mr. Jay Rodgers, Esq.
1277 Porter Rd
Flower Mound, TX 75022

Dear Mr. Rodgers:

Thank you for your recent phone call regarding your client's desire to possibly give The National Association for the Advancement of Colored People ("NAACP") a gift of stock.

Please feel free to contact our Chief Development Officer, Tammy Hawley at (410) 580-5617 to further discuss this potential gift.

Please do not hesitate to contact me at (410) 580-5792 should you require further assistance.

Very truly yours,

Angela Ciccolo
Deputy General Counsel

AC/sdm

CC: Tammy Hawley

The sum result was that having drastically changed their BATNA, they bought Norm out for more than he and I had agreed he would accept.

The second valuable lesson I learned occurred during one of the fascinating professor-led exercises at the Harvard OPM Program called "Two Pay Auction." In the exercise, we entrepreneur students engaged in an auction for a single $50 bill. Under the rules of the auction, a participant could only increase each bid by $1, and the party who won the auction received the $50 bill. The party who finished in second place was required to pay the amount of his final, failed bid and he received nothing. As the bidding neared the face amount of the $50 bill, it became clear that the final two bidders (everyone else had dropped out) would end up paying significantly more than fifty dollars for the $50 bill based on their desire to minimize their losses. As I recall, the winner paid $75 for the $50 bill, and the loser ponied up $74 for finishing second. The exercise was intended to demonstrate the dangers of gradualism.

The Harvard professor explained that falling prey to gradualism was the cause of our losing the Vietnam War. He noted that the political, rather than military, policy of gradual escalation emboldened our enemy to "up" the bidding by ever greater military action and at the same time served to discourage us when our "gradual escalation" policy yielded less than satisfactory results.

Some years later, I recalled this lesson when I was on the Denton County Courthouse steps bidding on a commercial property that the sheriff was auctioning at a foreclosure sale. My only remaining opponent hesitantly and repeatedly raised my bid by $100. After each raise, I immediately raised his bid by $2,000. My immediate and aggressive responses caused him to lose heart, and I bought the property for $97,000. Rental income from the property recovered my entire investment in three years. In the fourth year, I sold the property for over $500,000.

THE LESSON:

♦   *If you're going to jump in, do it with decisive action. My personal translation is, "Get big or get out."*

ENTREPRENEURIAL
REFLECTIONS

31

BUSINESS DOESN'T HAVE TO BE PERSONAL

T*he Godfather* is considered by many to be the greatest American film ever made. Among the many quotable lines, one stands out. "It's not personal…It's strictly business" as the rationale for killing rivals is a classic line known to almost all movie goers. If you're in the Mafia, this may work, but it's a foreign concept to those of us who don't make money by literally killing our competitors.

Business can be emotional, and by being emotional it can become personal. The challenge lies in preventing business from becoming personal while at the same time remaining consistent with the business principles each of us establishes in conducting our business lives.

I have been involved in three national banks as an investor/board member/chairman of the loan committee. That one bank was United Commerce Bank; I say three banks because United Commerce Bank was, is, and will remain (1) my first bank involvement, (2) my last bank involvement, and (3) my only bank involvement.

As one of the original investors and board members and having opened the bank in the mid-80s, we had many wild and exciting moments, battles with the regulators, and other crises. By 1991, the board was down from fourteen to a very functional seven members. As it happened, I had played a major role in attracting all but one of the seven board members to the bank. All of us were close friends.

I decided it was time to sell the bank. When I presented the idea, I was absolutely shocked to discover that all but one of my fellow directors and close friends were completely opposed to selling. The fight that followed ended up strengthening our bonds of friendship because we all retained our respect for one another. And, although vicious, it was a fight that no one lost.

The other director that was in favor of selling (Robert Fielder) and I both resigned from the board. I sought out and found a bank in a nearby larger city that wanted to buy our bank. I felt certain the shareholders at the upcoming annual meeting would be in favor of the sale and overshadow the board's desire. I was sure I had everything going my way, but the board had a trick up their sleeves, too. Although the sale got approved at the annual meeting, the board declared a cash dividend that reduced the assets of the bank by 15%. The almost laughable outcome was that the buyer honored his original offer despite the reduced value of the bank, and we all walked away friends with the additional money in our pocket as a result of our most honorable and enjoyable fight.

Less than two years after the sale, the directors who had opposed selling the bank opened a new bank within a mile of the one we sold. They even invited me to join as a founding director. I expressed my appreciation but told them I had already had a lifetime's supply of banks and bank regulators.

This experience was a bit like my time in the Army. I never want to do it again, but I sure enjoy looking back on it. To this day, when I'm about to get in a business fight, I remind myself that it's only business; it's not personal, and that maintaining my ethics and integrity are paramount.

THE LESSON:

◆ *If you maintain your ethics and integrity, you can disagree on business issues without destroying personal relationships.*

ENTREPRENEURIAL
REFLECTIONS

32

KNOW YOUR

STAKEHOLDERS

I was approached by an acquaintance, Bennie, who had been employed in the continuous-forms printing business for many years. The company he worked for had recently been acquired, and the buyer's changes were making the company an unpleasant place to work. Bennie told me that he and two others with a different continuous-forms printing company wanted to start a business to compete with their former employers. Their desire was legitimate, because none was bound by a noncompetition covenant.

I told them that, in order for me to help them start a company and invest alongside them, they would have to have "skin in the game." I defined skin in the game as each of them investing $20,000. Because all three were working men and had presumably saved little of their wages, I believed that the endeavor would end with this threshold requirement. However, I received a call some time later from Bennie. He announced that one of them had cashed in his 401(k) and paid the 10% penalty to raise his $20,000. Another had sold his house and moved into an apartment. Finally, Bennie had remarried his ex-wife and convinced her to dedicate the money she had gotten from him in their divorce to the new business venture. They had called my bluff, and I agreed to put up an additional $150,000.

Printing companies are traditionally low leveraged, capital intensive businesses. However, we found an equipment manufacturer that had recently repossessed a million and a half dollars' worth of near new printing equipment. Because they were highly motivated, we were able to buy it with no money down, no payments for six months, and ½ payments for the second six months. Additionally, we convinced a large paper supplier to put $250,000 in paper inventory on the floor of our new facility and give us 120 day terms. We no doubt set the record for being the most highly leveraged company in the industry.

Enroute to a meeting with our paper supplier one day, I asked Bennie if he knew who the biggest stakeholder in our newly formed business was. Bennie said, "Why, you are Jay." At that point, we were pulling into the paper company's parking lot, and I changed the subject. When we arrived at the CEO's office, I asked him if he knew who the biggest stakeholder in our company was. He responded, "You're damned right I do. I am." My friend Bennie never forgot that lesson. I am happy to report that all three of the working founders retired as millionaires.

THE LESSON:

◆   *Take time to know your stakeholders and look at the business through their eyes.*

ENTREPRENEURIAL
REFLECTIONS

33
PICK YOUR
FIGHTS CAREFULLY

As mentioned in a previous chapter, my friend Norm is the holder of 40 plus patents, and like other patent holders, he is occasionally involved in patent litigation. One particular patent fight with a competitor was particularly galling, and Norm called me to get my input and guidance. As the case proceeded, we reached a point where Norm could pay his adversary $200,000 and walk away with everything he had hoped to achieve. I encouraged him to write the check, call it a "win," and move on. Norm flatly refused to take my advice; pride was involved. Like many extremely wealthy individuals, Norm was prepared to spend extravagant amounts of money to insure that he prevailed. Another six months into the fight, Norm did indeed prevail on all counts. When the fight was over, Norm cheerfully informed me that his adversary had to pay him $200,000. Norm proudly held out his chest as the victor.

However, from the time Norm could have paid $200,000 and gotten everything he wanted until he got what he wanted and received $200,000, his legal bill had gone up by well over $400,000.

The extremely wealthy can afford to spend that kind of money on ego and/or principles. Can you? I have actually written three negotiated settlement checks when I felt I had an 80% chance of winning a lawsuit. Why?

1. Lawsuits are time consuming. They take you away from your core business.

2. Lawsuits are negative. Life is short, and a positive environment is worth a lot.

3. The only sure winners are the lawyers. The outcome is not always "just," but the lawyers get paid regardless.

I have met with many entrepreneurs who think a patent is total protection for their unique product. It isn't! Unless you have extremely deep pockets, you may well go broke defending your patent. In my experience, patent litigation is the most expensive litigation of all.

THE LESSON:

◆ *Choose your fights carefully. Are they really worth the time, effort, and expense?*

34
DEFINING YOUR MARKET –
THE CIRCLE MARKETING PLAN

I n a service business, defining your market upfront is one of the keys to profitability. Because the time and expense of employee travel to customer locations can be a significant cost to your business, it's important to distinguish between the desirability of certain business and the circumstances under which you will accept less desirable (less profitable) business.

In an in-home, non-medical assisted living business I started with my sister-in-law Becci, we drew two concentric circles around the company's headquarters, which we located within our primary market in select Dallas zip codes where wealthy older residents lived. Within the first circle, we marketed by direct mail and accepted any staffing assignment- even one and two hour unprofitable jobs with new customers. Additionally, we spent major time and money interviewing clients and insuring that we matched the client with the most appropriate caregiver for their personality and needs. Within the second circle, we did not expend money to market but would accept minimum four-hour assignments that came to us by referral or word-of-mouth. Outside the two circles, we would accept business only at negotiated rates which were immediately profitable for our company. In this manner, we directed our marketing efforts to the area we most desired to serve, therefore limiting the costs of expanding beyond that core market only to those situations most profitable to us. Within the first circle we became the provider of choice and frequently had clients ask us to raise our fees so that their caregiver would get a raise.

THE LESSON:

◆ *Define your market on the front-end, and don't lose money trying to be all things to all people.*

35
NAME IT
AND TAG IT RIGHT

Naming your company and adopting an effective tagline deserves a great deal more attention than it frequently receives. When naming a small or startup business, don't be led astray by the names of major corporations. Coca-Cola is a good name only because at this point virtually all of the world's population recognizes it.

Unfortunately, there's a big temptation to substitute initials for the name of a business. IBM gets away with this because most of the business world recognizes International Business Machines, Inc. The Entrepreneurs' Organization, a worldwide organization for entrepreneurs with chapters in forty countries, has fallen into the bad habit of calling themselves E.O. Using the initials rather than the name of the organization is, in my opinion, a huge mistake. It's very convenient for all those who are familiar with Entrepreneurs' Organization, but it offers absolutely no meaning to the people they want to attract as new members. You must maintain a constant vigil to prevent initials from replacing your company name. One startup that

I originally had total voting control of we named Physician Staffing Resources. We started the company with the CEO and one paid assistant. Today, the company has 325 employees. Despite my best efforts, the company's functional name is PSR.

When George Eastman founded Kodak, he intended it to be a worldwide company and therefore picked a name that was easy to pronounce in most languages, was pronounced the same in all languages, and had no negative connotations in any language. Hopefully you'll devote as much thought to naming your company as George did.

After we started an in-home non-medical assisted living business in Nashville, TN with my sister-in-law, we named the company Elderly Services, Inc. I like company names that help people understand what the company does or sells. Originally, I thought Elderly Services, Inc. was a brilliant name. Unfortunately, much to my chagrin, when we opened up for business, we quickly learned that nobody becomes "elderly" until about twenty minutes before they die. Our tagline "stay in charge and at home - never spend a single night in a nursing home" was some help in mitigating the disaster of our chosen name. We did manage to prosper, but it was no thanks to the name.

We sold the company which we had started with just a few thousand dollars for over a million dollars three years later. When we sold, we agreed to a non-compete in the Nashville market. Therefore, we opened our next in-home staffing facility in the Dallas, TX market. Having learned the painful naming lesson well, we named the new venture "Family Staffing Solutions." I'm happy to report that

Family Staffing Solutions became many, many times more successful than Elderly Services, Inc.

My wife Bettye and I started another company whose name worked very well. It was an ignition interlock device company that put a unit on cars that was normally ordered by the court as a requirement for convicted DUI and DWI offenders to legally drive. The device required them to blow into a unit measuring their breath alcohol before the car would start. We named this company Smart Start, Inc., and the logo was a stylized traffic light with the green, yellow and red circles.

When we started the company, MADD, Mothers Against Drunk Driving, still believed that all drunk drivers should be thrown in jail and the cell key thrown away. (As a side note, MADD created a very effective name by using initials.) Smart Start played a significant role in convincing MADD and the judicial system that it was neither cost-effective nor socially desirable to use lengthy incarceration as a solution to drunk driving. Attempting to reform the large population of longtime heavy drinkers was also not a practical approach.

We promoted the fact that the goal was to save lives being lost in traffic accidents caused by alcohol. It wasn't necessary to change their drinking habits to accomplish the goal. All we needed to do was to make sure they did not drive when drinking. This thinking brought about the tagline for Smart Start - *Separating Drinking from Driving.* Having played a major role in over twenty startups, the Smart Start tagline is, in my opinion, by far the best I have ever written.

Focus on sales and marketing value when you're naming your

company or writing taglines. Think of your prospective customers and how they will be impacted by the name and/or tag line.

THE LESSON:

♦   *Get it right. Choose a tagline and logo that is simple, memorable, and descriptive.*

36
GET CREATIVE

In 1995, Bettye and I organized a tour of the Greek Isles and ancient Ephesus (near Kusadasi, Turkey) with two dozen of our friends. Our commitment to attend a godchild's wedding in the United States necessitated our leaving the group a day early when we docked at Crete. Rough seas caused us to dock earlier than scheduled in Crete, so we arrived at Crete's small airport about 11a.m. and our flight to Athens wasn't until 7 p.m.

While standing near the Olympus Airline counter, I overheard the airline agent tell the couple ahead of me that, in addition to the 7 p.m. flight to Athens, they had one other, and it would depart in about 45 minutes; however, there was only one seat available on that flight. The couple indicated that they would not be interested in traveling to Athens separately and would wait for the 7 p.m. flight. When they left the ticket counter, I stepped up and was also told there was only one seat remaining on the early flight to Athens. I said, "That's perfect! My wife will take that last seat, and I'll take the jump seat in the cockpit." As I said this, I handed her my commercial pilot's license. (Please understand that the biggest plane I ever flew had ten seats.) The wall behind the agent had a door onto the tarmac and large plate glass windows that allowed us to see the 737 that would soon depart for Athens. The agent looked at my license, turned around, walked out onto the tarmac and up the rolling stairs on to the plane. She reappeared a minute or two later, and when she came back to the counter said, "That will be fine."

Bettye and I caught the early flight from Crete to Athens and made it home to the United States in time for the wedding. The pilots were great guys. They pointed out the sites to me and invited Bettye and me to dinner that evening.

This all happened because I did a little creative thinking and, more importantly, **ASKED**. Remember the worst thing that can happen in situations like this is they say "no," and that leaves you even, not down.

The Lesson:

♦   *If you're not getting a lot of "no's," you're missing a lot of "yes's."*

37
"No" IS A
GREAT STARTING PLACE

As mentioned in chapter 35, we sold out Smart Start to my hand-picked successor and another shareholder at a $15 million valuation. Bettye and I were approaching 70, and we were ready to change direction. I wrote my friends with stock advising them that we were selling out but that the company was headed to the moon, and I advised them to hold their stock. That business sold a few months ago for $340 million all cash. I am the first to applaud Lamar's success in continuing to grow Bettye's and my goal of separating drinking from driving. We take great pride in having created many millionaires and several multi-millionaires among our friends, employees, and investors as a result of starting Smart Start. Hard to believe that when we ended the first month we were open, we had only one customer.

With Smart Start behind us and the city pushing out to our ranch, we decided to move to town. We committed to buy a condominium unit in downtown Fort Worth. The project was still under construction as we were preparing to depart for Canada, the Calgary Stampede, and our extended annual summer vacation. Before leaving, I listed our ranch house north of Dallas/Fort Worth with a real estate agent. It was the summer of 2009, and the residential real estate market was truly in the tank. When we returned to Texas in late summer, one of the first things I did was call our real estate agent to get an update.

He informed me that the real estate market was dead and that he had only showed our place three times. He added that one of the couples that looked was really knocked out by the house, our hilltop location overlooking the Tour Eighteen golf course, and just about everything else. He went on to tell me that the prospects owned a home in Decatur, Texas and had decided not to do anything until their current home was sold.

I asked my real estate agent for the name and phone number of the couple's real estate agent. I assured him that, per our listing contract, he would be paid as stipulated. However, I asked him to stay out of my way regarding this couple that he had long since written off as prospects.

My next step was to call the couple's real estate agent. She was happy to arrange for her clients to make another trip to our ranch house. Before the day was out, we were scheduled to meet at our property the following day.

Less than 45 minutes after Mr. Rick Garrett and his wife Amy arrived with their real estate agent, we agreed that they would be the proud new owners of our five-acre estate. I made some concessions, but none that my real estate agent should not have pursued had he been doing his job. I accepted a price below the asking price; however, my real estate agent was aware that I would accept a much lower price. My only other significant concession came as a result of knowing that Rick wanted to sell his house prior to buying another one. I resolved this objection by suggesting that I give Rick a short term second loan in the amount of the equity he had in his present house. I agreed to make my loan at the lowest legal interest rate, at that time about 1%. The note would be due at the earlier of the closing date of the sale of his home, or in two years. As it turned out, Rick followed my example, lowered the asking price on their Decatur home, and as a result, sold and closed on his house in about five months.

Rick and I have become great friends, and he is one of Biz Owners' Ed's valued mentors. I conduct all of my business so that after the closing, be it the sale of real estate or a business, the buyer and I frequently develop an ongoing friendly relationship. Many buyers of companies and other assets I have been involved in have become close friends. That only happens when you live by a win-win philosophy.

None of this would have been possible had I simply accepted the "No" Rick gave my real estate agent as final.

THE LESSON:

◆   *Use "No" as the starting point, not as the finish line.*

ENTREPRENEURIAL REFLECTIONS

38

THE REBATE

As mentioned in a previous chapter, before Bettye and I sold off most of the ranch and the ranch house, we were looking at buying a residence in Fort Worth. We contracted to buy a downtown Fort Worth condo being built above the newly opened Omni Hotel. Bob Rowling, the owner of the Omni sixty property hotel chain, had just started marketing the 87 condo units being built above the 15-story Omni Hotel as they were still several months away from completion. At that point, the residential real estate market was extremely hot. I was dragging my feet regarding committing to a unit and putting up a deposit. When the sales agent pressed, wanting to know why with our apparent strong interest we had not moved ahead, I explained that I was concerned that the market was overheated, the bubble might well burst, and they would need to lower prices. Because this project was by far the highest per square foot residential property in Ft. Worth, I thought it was especially vulnerable. I was immediately assured that Bob was funding the project out-of-pocket and would never lower the prices. My response was, "That's wonderful. I will get back to you tomorrow afternoon."

The next morning I met with David Hammer, my M&A attorney, and he drafted a beautiful clause for me that provided a rebate equal to any reduction in the current published unit prices. If a unit sold at a price 9% below the currently listed price, I would receive a check for 9% of my purchase price. If later a unit sold at a 14% reduction, I would receive another 5% and on and on. The next afternoon I met with the condo sales manager, and, much to my surprise, they agreed to include my clause in the contract. As I have said many times, "Ask and you may-shall-will receive."

When the market did fall, Mike, Bob's right hand man, contacted me and told me that Bob would like to buy out my clause. I offered to sell it for $172,500. I knew that although most units were being reduced only about 7%-9%, the least expensive unit in the project was being reduced from $399,000 to $299,000 as a loss leader and means of advertising "from $299,000." Later that week, Mike called. He explained that the previous night he and Bob had flown in from Houston on the company plane and had discussed my $172,500 offer. Mike told me that Bob wanted to counter and was prepared to pay $100,000. I simply said, "That's not acceptable. However, I'll be contacting the sales office tomorrow as I've decided to buy the $299,000 unit."

The next morning I got wind of a rumor at the Omni of which the gist was: "Good news! We have a buyer for the unit on the 16th floor. Bad news: Jay Rodgers is the buyer, and his net cost will be $35,000."

Later that morning, I got a call from Mike, asking if I was really serious about buying the second unit. My reply was, "Yes; under the circumstances, I feel it is the thing to do." After a pause, I continued. "However, I am willing to (at that point I could almost visualize Mike leaning closer to the phone) reopen my original offer for 24 hours."

I received a check for $172,500, and as a rebate (reduction in purchase price), it wasn't even subject to taxes.

I employed a similarly successful approach while selling Healthcare Staff Resources to Kimberly Quality Care. That story is told in Ch. 28 "Don't Lose Money Trying to Predict the Future."

THE LESSON:

◆   *The time to address your concerns is before you sign on the dotted line. Do your due diligence and look for ways to reduce your risk.*

ENTREPRENEURIAL
REFLECTIONS

39
BE WILLING TO
GIVE TOUGH ADVICE

I frequently tell people that all my friends are strong because the weak can't handle me. I have often thought about trying to soften my somewhat overly direct and harsh style, but I always conclude with, "Why the hell would I want a bunch of weak friends?"

When Tony Jeary and I were collaborating to write *Advice Matters*, one afternoon Tony turned to me and said, "Jay, you could make big bucks as a coach."

My reply was, "Yes, but then I would need to be nice to people just because they have a big check book." I know myself well enough to know that I cannot candy coat the truth, and I am much better at tough love than playing nice.

One example of my style of tough love occurred several years ago when I was serving on a Denton, TX Grand Jury. During a break, I was surprised when one of the jurors asked me if I would be willing to help her with her business. When I inquired as to why she asked me, she told me that three people had suggested that I was the one she needed to approach for help.

As is my custom, I agreed to have one session at my office. I always use initial sessions to gather the facts and decide if I can be of help and, if so, whether I want to become involved. Jane had operated a very successful cake and candy business for over twenty years. Her primary focus was wedding cakes. Over the past three years, her profits had dwindled to near non-existent, and Jane had reached the point of hating to get up and go to work.

We had a good meeting and I agreed to sign on. One of Jane's first questions was how much I charged. I explained that normally I did not charge; however, in her case, it would cost her candy and cake.

At our next meeting, I had studied her overall operations and financials and concluded that step one was for her to raise her prices. When I told her she immediately needed to raise her prices by 20%, she protested that she would lose all of her customers. My response was that she had sought me out because she was slowly going broke and half-jokingly told her, "Let's get it over with." When she left my office, she had agreed to raise her prices 20% across the board.

She did lose a small number of customers. But, with the additional 20% of revenue hitting her bottom line, she again became profitable almost overnight. She arrived for our third session absolutely elated and said, "Oh Jay, you were right. I'll do anything you tell me." I told her that step two was not going to be as easy. And again she said, "I'll do anything." I explained that an employee that had been with her from day one had to go. This employee was creating a lot of problems, and the final straw was that the employee had involved her new husband somewhat in the business. Amidst the flow of emotion and tears, Jane finally asked, "Is there a compromise?"

She immediately brightened up when I said, "Of course." The smile faded when I explained that as long as she dismissed the employee, banned her from the premises and changed the locks, if she wanted to, she could continue to send the employee a check. Jane reluctantly accepted my advice and dismissed the employee. Several months later, she confided that this second piece of advice had been even more valuable than raising her prices.

Several years have now passed. Jane remains profitable, has expanded her business, and we remain good friends. I'm delighted with her success and glad that I was able to help. As I was preparing to publish this book, I sent a draft of "Tough Advice" to Jane for her approval and permission to include it. Below is her response.

> I loved it just the way you wrote it. You could also say that when I saw your name on caller ID I broke into a sweat for the first few years. When I talk about you, I tell people that I never ask you anything unless I want the truth. and sometimes the truth is not what I want to hear but what I need to hear.
>
> You truly changed my life. and more specifically. my business life. Thanks for that. I love and respect you and Bettye so much.
>
> Jane

THE LESSON:

◆　*Don't be afraid to give or get tough advice.*

40
ACTIVELY PURSUE
THE TALENT YOU NEED

Many of my companies had experienced ongoing difficulties in identifying and hiring qualified sales personnel. Because I believe that you can't pay a good salesman too much, I knew our difficulties were not with our pay structure. Rather, we didn't do a good job in qualifying our prospective employees.

I was in Las Vegas one day attending a seminar on sales. One of the speakers was a Dallas man named Tom. Tom talked about the importance of pre-employment testing to determine if an individual was likely to succeed in sales. His presentation impressed me, and I believed that he could help us solve our longstanding problem with the lackluster performance of, and the resulting turnover among, our sales staff.

When Tom completed his presentation, I approached the platform and asked him if I might take a few minutes of his time. Tom replied that he was headed to the airport right away to return home to Dallas. I asked if I might join him on his cab ride to the airport so we could talk further. He agreed, and we talked all the way to the airport. When we arrived, I felt there was still more to learn, so I changed my return ticket and joined him. When we boarded the plane, I persuaded the person sitting next to Tom to change seats with me. By the time we landed, Tom was on the team. Ever since then, Tom has screened and interviewed all of our sales candidates, and the results have been spectacular. Additionally, Tom donates his time and talent as a powerful guest speaker at our Biz Owners' Ed program.

THE LESSON:

◆   *Seize the moment. As my Welsh friend taught me, "Cut a walking stick when you find it."*

41
BE THE BIGGEST
RISK TAKER IN YOUR DEALS

There's a disturbing pattern in America today to use other people's money for everything. We see that pattern in Congress, in charities (where many times way too much of the money goes to the staff rather than to the charitable purpose for which it was purportedly raised) and, sadly, in entrepreneurship.

I have always taken the position that I owe it to my investors to take the biggest financial risk in every business venture that I launch. If I'm using somebody else's money, I want them to know that I'll suffer the biggest loss if we fail. And, I want them to be assured that we are equally yoked in the venture and will win or lose together. I take no management or promotional fee and use no other gimmick to boost my return at the expense of my investors. It is the alignment of my interests with the interests of my investors that has allowed me to participate alongside the same core group of investors for decades and to continue to count all of them as friends through both wins and losses. For the past 48 years, a few phone calls have been all that has been needed to raise money for a new venture.

Once your business is experiencing success, the natural tendency is to increase the amount of your salary, sometimes even to astronomical levels. Your paychecks can become extremely expensive when it's time to sell your company. Equally expensive is the practice of living off the company. By this I mean running many personal expenses through the company as business expenses – entertainment, travel, personal vehicles, insurance, family employee paychecks, etc. Using the rule of thumb that small private businesses are worth 4-5 times earnings, each dollar you siphon from the company's annual earnings will cost $4-$5 when you sell the company. Yes, recasting plays a role, but dirty books are dirty books.

While it's true that your prospective buyer may attempt to recast the company's earnings to show the business's actual bottom line, the higher you set the compensation bar for the function you perform, the easier it becomes for the buyer to do likewise. Typically, the buyer will have some concerns about how important your role in the company is to its success. Again, the higher the compensation, the more concern. If you absolutely must have more money, borrow it from the company at the lowest legal interest rate and pay the loan off with capital gains dollars at the closing table when the business sells. If the personal expenses you have run through the company are well-hidden, they won't be recast. If they are not well-hidden, the IRS may want to talk to you. The cleaner your books are the last three years prior to sale, the more capital gains dollars you can expect to receive for the company.

THE LESSON:

- *Don't allow short-term benefits to be detrimental to your game winning homerun.*

ENTREPRENEURIAL
REFLECTIONS

42

BEWARE THE
ONE TRICK PONY

My long-time friend John invested in a computer software company which provided a management and accounting program for college and university dormitories. It covered both student and outside summer resident groups. The company's underlying technology was sound, but the company was bedeviled by the lengthy sales cycle associated with public and private colleges and universities. It was not unusual for this company to call on its prospective customers for five years and even longer before concluding a sale. The CEO jokingly talked about prospective academic institutions that belonged to their five-year club. Because they sold only the one software product, the cost of producing a sale was devastating to their profitability.

John convinced me to get involved when he offered me 20% of the company stock to join the board and focus on their success. It did not take long to determine that the sales expense had to be drastically reduced if they were to become profitable. The two options I focused on for accomplishing that were (1) adding several much less expensive items to their product line that could be sold to the same academic prospects on a first or second call basis, or (2) selling the company to a well-established organization that was already calling on our prospects and sold a wide range of products. We settled on the latter option. A buyer was identified, a sale was concluded, and the company's technology finally had a real chance to succeed in the market.

THE LESSON:

♦ *Be careful if you have a one-trick pony. Success often eludes the one-trick pony. Look for more tricks or another buyer.*

43

SHOP AROUND EVEN WHILE BEING A LOYAL CUSTOMER

I was understandably excited about owning my first Lexus. A high-end luxury vehicle is a source of joy to any car aficionado. Its bells and whistles offer countless opportunities for amazement, amusement and even frustration at their complexities. I bought my first Lexus (a 1990 model) from a Fort Worth dealer in 1989, the year Lexus was introduced in the U.S. The magnitude of the expense did, however, make me wonder if I might have purchased at a better price in another market. On a flight to London the following year, I found myself seated next to Carl Sewell, the owner of one of the most successful Lexus dealerships in North Texas and author of *Customers for Life*. Our conversation naturally turned to my Lexus and the fact that I was intending to trade it for another new Lexus sedan next year. Carl made it clear that the Sewell Lexus policy was to rely on its well-deserved reputation for customer service as the basis for holding the line on the purchase price of each and every vehicle. I got the clear impression that the demand for Lexus vehicles in the DFW market was so strong that none of the dealers were offering much of a price concession.

When the time came to purchase my second Lexus, I dutifully collected quotes from Sewell Lexus and two other North Texas Lexus dealerships. All the quotes were within $500.00 of each other. In the midst of shopping for my new car, I flew to San Antonio on an overnight business trip. After the meeting, I was in my hotel room early with time on my hands. In those days, the hotel rooms still had *Yellow Pages* and I ended up looking up the local Lexus dealership. The dealership had just changed hands, and I was fortunate enough to get the new General Manager on the phone. When I asked him if he was serious about selling cars, he explained that his company had just acquired the dealership, the lot was overflowing, and he was extremely serious. I told him in that case, on my way to the airport the next day, I would have the cab make a small detour and stop at his dealership. This was in 1991. When I stopped, I told the cab to wait.

Less than five minutes after I shook hands with the new manager, I had purchased my new Lexus. He set the allowance for my trade-in based on its mileage and my description of its condition. I told him that he could deduct from the trade-in allowance any amount he thought was appropriate after he saw the car. He accepted my proposal, and the following week my new car was delivered to me at my office north of Dallas. He didn't request any deductions after seeing my car, and I purchased that car for $5,000 less than my best DFW offer.

Since that time, I have purchased over fifty new Lexus from the dealer for myself, my wife, my attorney, my CPA, and a couple of other close friends, all of which the dealership has delivered to Dallas. Service is important, but sometimes it pays to shop around.

Being a loyal customer also has its perks as I found out when I needed a new pickup. Because I had been so happy with all of my Lexus vehicles (made by Toyota), I decided to buy a new Toyota pickup. Shortly after taking delivery, Bettye pointed out that my new truck was leaking oil on our driveway. I returned the truck to the dealer. As it turned out, the camshaft had not been properly installed and major repairs would be required. The dealer informed me that they would have it repaired within a few days. My response was, "Fix it, like hell you will. I paid for a new truck, and I want a new truck." The dealer responded that they just couldn't do that. I told them to hold the truck, do nothing to it without my authorization, and that I would send them further instructions from my office that afternoon.

When I returned to my office, I pulled out the records on the, at that time, forty plus Lexus I had been involved in purchasing. I faxed the list complete with VIN numbers of each vehicle to the dealership. I'm sure you won't find it hard to believe that the next morning they called to inform me that they would be delivering a brand new truck to my office that day.

THE LESSON:

◆   *Leverage your loyalty.*

ENTREPRENEURIAL REFLECTIONS

44

THERE'S ALWAYS
A MARKET FOR THE BEST

My friend Claude, whom I originally met at the Harvard OPM program, shared with me that earlier in his business life, after achieving considerable success, he fell on hard times and nearly went broke. Determined to survive, Claude made the decision to fire-sale his antique car collection, his art collection, and everything else he owned that wasn't essential.

What Claude discovered in the process provides a lesson that I consider very valuable. He told me that because he had to sell out virtually overnight to raise cash, he was not in a position to demand or receive top dollar on his assets. He said the very finest of the cars in his collection and the prized pieces in his art collection, the assets he had extravagantly paid top dollar for, were sold immediately and for significant profit. The so-so cars and the okay art were harder to sell and sold at a loss. One example he used was a pencil drawing he had by Picasso. Even though it was an original Picasso, the art community didn't consider it one of his finer works. Claude even lost money on that.

Every time I make a luxury investment purchase, I think of
Claude's fire sale and walk away if I can't afford to buy the very best.

THE LESSON:

- *There's always a market for excellence and quality.*

45

YOU CANNOT
CREATE A MARKET

Without a doubt, one of the most valuable lessons I learned during the Harvard OPM program was from Professor Marty Marshall. He convinced all of us in the class that you cannot create a market. You can only serve one.

Ford's disastrous attempt to sell the Edsel is a great example of this wisdom. Typically, the most incredibly successful entrepreneurs identify a market that's not being served or is not being served well and move in to properly serve it. A good example is Levi Strauss, an immigrant who responded to the fact that California miners were so rough on their pants that they couldn't find pants strong enough to withstand the abuse of their work. Strauss originally used canvas which was too harsh and settled on denim which became an overnight success.

Another perhaps less obvious but outstanding opportunity lies in identifying a market that is being poorly served and serving it well. One such opportunity was found in public restrooms everywhere.

Introduced in 1948, the World Dryer survived unchallenged for over 50 years. It sold for, depending on the model, around $300. Every entrepreneur that ever used one, and that unfortunately includes me, should be absolutely ashamed of not immediately seeing the incredible opportunity that this high priced, inefficient, miserable piece of equipment offered. It was so bad that under the instructions that told you to "rub hands briskly in air stream" someone would frequently add, "wipe hands on pants after use." Any thinking individual should have realized that a $20 hairdryer would do a better job at a fraction of the cost. Fortunately, the Excel Dryer did recognize the opportunity, and they're rapidly replacing the World Dryer in public restrooms everywhere.

THE LESSON:

◆   *You can't create a market. Opportunity lies in identifying and serving unserved and underserved markets.*

46
DON'T PAY UNCLE SAM
TO START YOUR BUSINESS

Many young entrepreneurs put their money in their start-up business alongside investor money. They then immediately begin drawing a salary sufficient to support themselves. Your tax advisor may tell you that you need to take some salary. If so, take the absolute minimum amount required. Rather than putting your cash in the business, with either an LLC or Sub-S, you can buy your percent of the equity for a fraction of what the other investors pay. This allows you to put the rest of your funds aside and live on them free of payroll taxes. Likewise, you can loan the balance of the money to the company and live on the monthly repayment paying taxes only on the interest.

THE LESSON:

- *Understand the tax laws and understand your rights. You can live a good deal longer and/or better on the same income if Uncle Sam isn't sharing a big paycheck with you.*

47

AVOID THE SOFTWARE
DEVELOPMENT PROJECT

Technology can be a wonderful tool in two situations. First, the software must be capable of accomplishing the purpose for which you acquired it. Second, you (or your appropriate employee(s)) must be able to use it efficiently. For these reasons, I avoid what the tech people refer to as "bleeding edge" technology and leading edge technology. While some technophiles simply must have the latest, greatest anything, the extreme high cost, the productivity lost, the associated problems, and the longer learning curve frequently make it unprofitable. Business is, after all, about profit. If you doubt that, try giving your church a share of your losses. I believe in using technology that is proven to increase productivity. Only then should company resources be dedicated to training your employee base in its application to your business.

If at all possible, avoid falling into the trap of software development. If your business is large enough, somewhere in it there will be an IT person who knows he can build exactly what your company needs. Worse yet, your IT person may have an IT friend, or may have read about an IT developer, who can certainly build what you need. If you fall into this trap, forget about the metrics of "on time" and "under budget." You almost certainly will not experience either. And when you don't, the shininess of your new toy will dim significantly as time goes by and the cost overruns increase. When you buy software, buy results that are valuable to your company. I always say, "I'll pay you when I push a button and x happens…not when you tell me the marvelous things you have achieved." When you use software off of the shelf, a company supports it. When you contract to develop software specifically for your company, or even if you develop it internally, the developer being away on a fishing trip may shut down production, and one heart attack may destroy its ongoing value. That heart attack can potentially even leave the company in dire straits.

The Lessons:

♦ *Every new technology or advancement isn't necessarily a good deal. Evaluate software not based on the bells and whistles. Evaluate it based on your bottom line.*

♦ *Few businesses truly require custom software development. Yours, in all likelihood, is not one of them.*

48
KNOW WHEN
TO GET OUT OF THE WAY

My friend Jon has a business supplying parts and equipment for airport baggage conveyor systems. Jon even contracts to have some high-demand parts manufactured.

Although his business was parts and equipment for conveyor systems, Jon had everything necessary to build a conveyor system which he confessed to me was, from time to time, a major temptation when requests for proposals came across his desk. I pointed out to him that he had never assembled a complete, functioning system, had no experience in installation, and could incur significant expenses for an installation team to travel to, and reside at or near, the airport location of any system customer until the installation was complete and accepted by the airport. He would also have to deal with requirements from several unions including the electricians' union, and he would have to adhere to local codes and union rules. Despite my warnings, Jon finally succumbed to temptation and the promise of big dollars. He bid on and was awarded the contract to install a system on the East Coast. For the reasons about which I had already warned him, the job quickly became a financial disaster and was on the verge of bankrupting his otherwise successful company.

At that point, Jon came to me asking for help. I referred Fergus Reynolds, my CPA, to Jon, and we began putting together the kind of financial information about his parts and equipment business which confirmed what I intuitively knew: Jon's focus should be totally on parts and equipment. My CPA was able to determine the margins produced by individual parts and equipment. This information was extremely valuable in inventory management, deciding what parts to manufacture, and focusing on sales efforts. With the business focusing on parts and equipment and taking advantage of the detailed financial reports we were generating, the company rapidly returned to being financially solvent.

With the company turned around, I didn't hear from Jon for some time. When I did, Jon informed me that when he saw a request for proposal for a complete system that was very basic, temptation had again overwhelmed him. He was once again in financial trouble. I said, "Jon, I'll help you get out of the trap one more time, but only on one condition. You have to agree to turn over day-to-day control of the company to Colin (his stepson who was already active in the business). You can continue to be compensated as a director and consultant, but you have to agree to stay out of the day-to-day management of the business and sell nothing but parts and equipment. Additionally, for the foreseeable future, you need to give Collin your proxy to vote your share on all operational issues."

Jon somewhat reluctantly agreed. As part of the transition, Jon gifted Colin 10% ownership of the company.

We put out the fires, completed the disastrous system installation, and returned the business to its core mission. The company was financially weakened, but it had survived. Jon went home, built a nice shop on his acreage, and began pursuing his passion of restoring early 1900's motorcycles and selling parts for them which brought him enjoyment and success.

The business began to prosper. The next time Jon and I had a serious discussion about his business, he complained to me that Colin was making more money out of the business than Jon was. Jon also informed me that he had gifted Colin an additional 39% of the business, leaving their respective ownership positions at 51% and 49%. Unfortunately, I couldn't believe Jon had done that unilaterally and so limited his options to exit! Had he made me aware of his planned gift, I would have recommended a totally different approach. Let me explain. Most buyers for tax reasons want to buy the assets of a business because they're able to write off a significant portion of the purchase price as goodwill. A 2/3 vote of the shareholders was then required by Jon's company to authorize the sale of substantially all of its assets. Not only did Jon no longer have 67% of the stock, but he had also created a substantial minority owner with a vested financial interest in not selling. Jon had reached the age where he was ready to sell the company, but he could no longer count on the shareholder vote necessary to sell his own business in a structure where a potential buyer could likely be found.

Jon told Colin his intention and asked for an offer. Predictably, Colin offered to buy out Jon at such a ridiculously low valuation that it appeared there was no possibility to sell to him. I began to look for another buyer that would be willing to buy Jon's stock. Not long afterward, a friend called to tell me that he and a partner were looking for a business to buy. I introduced him to Jon, and Jon took my friend on a tour of the business and showed him the financials. My friend was prepared to buy Jon's ownership position in the business rather than all of the business assets, thereby freeing Jon from the need to secure Colin's vote to sell the company. Jon made Colin aware of the offer and his intention to accept it. Fortunately this put a great deal of pressure on Colin because the new 51% owner would take over as CEO putting Colin out of a job. Realizing his precarious position, Colin agreed to pay a comparable price for the business and asked only one concession: that Jon accept a note for 80% of the purchase price. Jon agreed with a condition of his own: Jon's shares and Colin's shares would be collateral for the note and would be delivered to Colin only when the note was fully paid. Until that time, Jon would be the sole director of the company. We then made it clear to Colin that any failure on his part to honor the terms of the note would result in his termination as CEO and Jon's foreclosure on all of the ownership interest in the business which was pledged as collateral for the purchase price. The parties agreed, and Jon and I then turned our attention to selling the land and building so that Colin could move the business to less expensive quarters.

As Jon's real estate agent, I had been negotiating with a very difficult individual for several months who was a prospect to buy Jon's land and building. After receiving several unacceptable contracts and having convinced Jon to walk away from the most recent offer without countering, I was finally able to negotiate a clean contract to sell the land and building. With Colin wanting to move the company, the timing was perfect. I immediately called Jon and said, "If I can hand you a perfectly clean contract for $1.1 million all cash, will you accept it?"

After hemming and hawing, Jon said that he would. I said, "Good, because I have a no-contingency contract on my desk for $1.2 Million."

We closed on the sale of the land and building, and we closed on the sale of the business to Colin. Jon is now enjoying his small antique motorcycle business and semi-retirement. I'm sure Jon enjoys looking back on finally succeeding in building and selling a successful business which provides him with a comfortable retirement. Had he not been smart enough to step aside when he did, that never would have happened.

THE LESSON:

◆ *Know when to step aside. I've seen a lot of entrepreneurs who built great businesses but ended up destroying them by not stepping aside at the right time. Be careful that you're not one of them.*

ENTREPRENEURIAL
REFLECTIONS

49

YOUR TIME IS VALUABLE

When we started Physician Staffing Resources, we originally assisted hospital administrators in making certain that their emergency rooms had an adequate number of properly trained and credentialed emergency physicians.

I had assembled and represented the investor group, and I was, as always, the single largest investor. Although I was not personally involved on a daily basis, I felt a responsibility to the investors I had encouraged to participate.

My partner was doing a great job of managing the contracts we had, and each contract produced a good gross profit. However, we needed more contracts to be bottom line profitable. Looking at the financial statements, it was obvious that our sales expense was exorbitant – airfare, hotels, and entertainment. Added to that was the time required to travel to hospitals nationally, assess the needs of the potential client, and prepare a proposal. We were only closing a deal in about one-in-six trips.

I believed that many of the requests for proposals came from administrators who had already decided on another provider or course of action but just wanted our proposal as a bargaining tool. We studied and discussed the problem at length and came up with what proved to be an outstanding solution.

We responded to all future RFP's by saying we were unwilling to reply to any RFP without thoroughly evaluating the needs of the hospital and the community. This typically took one or two days on site and the charge was $2,500 per day plus expenses. We added that if the potential client did not find our evaluation report to be worth more than they paid for it, we would not submit a bill. (No hospital ever asked to not be billed.)

We assured our potential clients that the report would be extremely helpful whether they hired us or another provider. In the event that we were the successful bidder, the cost of the evaluation would be credited back on future invoices.

From the day we began the program and its policies, we made far fewer sales trips, our close rate soared, and we became profitable.

THE LESSON:

♦ *Your time is valuable. Don't be afraid to disrupt an industry's current processes in favor of a better one. This philosophy applies to every industry.*

50

PUT ALL YOUR
EGGS IN ONE BASKET

Diversification is touted as a tried and true principle in investment management. That classic portfolio theory suggests that the prudent investor allocates his investable wealth over a diversified array of assets such as stocks, bonds, commodities, precious metals, and real estate. In recent years, the list has expanded to include foreign equities. Diversification is designed to reduce risk; however, I believe it is guaranteed to reduce the size of your win.

You have probably heard the story of the general who sailed to a foreign land with all his troops. After disembarking, the troops looked back to see all three of their ships fully engulfed in flames. The general announced that they were there to conquer or perish.

Just like the general, when you're fully committed and your future depends on it, your odds of winning go up dramatically.

I speak with many young entrepreneurs who would like to start their own businesses but are afraid to leave the supposed security of their current jobs. Their excuse is that they would if they did not have a spouse and children to provide for. Fortunately, unlike the general's troops, even if they risk it all and fail, they won't perish. Better to try and fail than die never knowing if your vision would have taken you to the moon. Paychecks are addictive and a major barrier on the road to wealth creation. Young entrepreneurs should ignore "don't put all your eggs in one basket." Typically:

1. They have a small net worth and very little to lose.

2. Most of their assets are bankruptcy proof.

3. They have a lifetime to rebuild.

4. They have the energy to ensure their family will continue to have a roof over their head and three meals a day.

If you want to win the lottery, you have got to buy a ticket. In my opinion, young entrepreneurs that see an opportunity should put all of their eggs in one basket, focus on that basket, and give it tender loving care.

At 76, conventional wisdom says I should be financially conservative, invest in bonds, and avoid risks. Prudent? Yes, but being a serial entrepreneur, when I find a deal that I believe will be a major winner, I still occasionally put way too many eggs in one basket. A good example is Applied DNA Sciences, Inc. Four years ago, when I first became acquainted with Applied DNA Sciences, it was an over-the-counter penny stock. I studied the company, watched it closely, become acquainted with top management, and, by the time they were listed on the NASDAQ, had invested just over a million dollars in their stock (more than I have ever before or since invested in a company I did not control). Since then, they have experienced many of the trials and tribulations of growing companies. The market value of my investment has ranged from a paper profit of $1,000,000 to a loss of over $400,000. Today, 8/25/16, the company stock (APDN) closed at $2.95, and their warrants (APDNW), expiring 11/17/19 and allowing the holder to buy one share of stock for each warrant at $3.50, closed at $1.01. As this manuscript goes to print, I am down $334,442.80.

My friends suggested I not provide the hard numbers shown above. They were afraid that if the company does not do well, I'll look bad. My answer? Facts are facts. Entrepreneurs take calculated risks, and I continue to believe that this company will go to the moon. If I'm wrong, I'm wrong. It's not a sin.

THE LESSON:

◆ *Entrepreneurs take calculated risks. I'd rather risk losing than forfeit the opportunity to win. If you're way over the hill like me, it's a great way to keep a little excitement in your life.*

ENTREPRENEURIAL
REFLECTIONS

51

DON'T FORGET TO ASK!

In the early 80s after several successful ventures, I was finally ready to build my dream house – a ranch house situated on the highest point in the area overlooking my ranch. I installed Kohler's Rochelle commodes in all bathrooms and the matching bidet in the master. At that time, I think the Rochelle low silhouette toilet was the most expensive commode that Kohler offered. Because I served as my own general contractor on numerous building projects, I frequently attended the National Home Builder's show. Three or four years after the ranch house was complete, I was at the show in Vegas. When I entered the Kohler exhibit, I asked a representative the name of the top ranking Kohler executive that was currently in the exhibit. He said, "Well, today, that would be Mr. Kohler." He motioned towards two gentlemen conversing, indicating that Mr. Kohler was the gentleman on the left.

I walked over and stood nearby while they finished their conversation. When the visitor turned to leave, I immediately stepped forward and said, "Mr. Kohler, I'd like to speak to you."

I explained to him that I had already had to replace the four

Rochelle commode seats because the bright Texas sun streaming in through the windows had turned the seats a yellowish color, and the replacements were already beginning to turn yellow. It wouldn't have been a big deal, but even back in the 80's, the wholesale price on these seats was well over $100 each. The Rochelle commodes were so designed that no other seats would substitute. I explained that while the Texas sun was indeed extremely bright, a product that carried the Kohler name and an extremely high price tag should retain its bright white color indefinitely.

With that, Mr. Kohler reached into his pocket, pulled out a business card, and wrote on the back:

 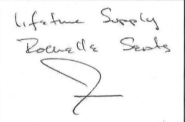

Lesson:

◆ *If you don't ask, you cannot receive.*

52

MY HERO

While I was operating the Ranchland summer youth horsemanship ranch, Gordon McClendon (builder of a national communications empire) had Cielo Ranch near me north of Dallas. One wing of the main ranch house was the John Wayne suite. I frequently provided horses when Gordon had more guests than his stable could accommodate. As a result, I was invited to a major party at Cielo Ranch the night before John Wayne's movie *Chisum* premiered in Dallas. I was standing near the pool when John stepped out of his quarters and was immediately surrounded by guests. As luck would have it, I ended up standing directly in front of John, not much more than arm's length away. When there was a momentary silence, I looked up, and said, "Mr. Wayne, I've got to talk to you."

The legend replied, "Speak on, little man."

"I've got 50 youngsters who want to meet you," I said, and told him about our youth ranch.

Although obviously tipsy, he immediately replied, "Well, bring 'em in to our parade in the morning, and I'll meet them."

I immediately headed back to my ranch, and by 4 a.m. had arranged to haul seventy head of horses and a surrey with a fringe on top complete with a sign welcoming Mr. Wayne to Dallas. With my staff and all the youngsters in their Ranchland logo shirts, as we stood along the parade route, I was wondering if he imbibed so much the night before that he wouldn't even remember our conversation. About that time, a Cadillac convertible came by heading to the near-by start of the parade. When John Wayne saw our group, he tapped the driver on the shoulder, had him do a u-turn and pulled up to the curb next to us. He got out, shook every single youngsters hand, and then called a parade official over and instructed him that he wanted half of our group in front of his car and half of the group behind it. It sure is nice to find out that some legends really are.

If you don't ask for what you want, you won't get what you want.

I wouldn't be able to tell this story now if I'd been too timid to approach John Wayne.

THE LESSON:

◆   *As mentioned before, great things happen
    when you ask.*

ENTREPRENEURIAL
REFLECTIONS

APPENDIX

BIZ OWNERS' ED

Biz Owners' Ed (Biz) was created because a small group of highly successful entrepreneurs believed in small business and the benefits it provides to America's economy and society. This group knew there were numerous entrepreneurs out there who shared their belief and who were willing and eager to give back to, help perpetuate, and help expand this country's seriously committed entrepreneurs by sharing advice from lessons they had learned.

The idea for Biz Owners' Ed was originally conceived by Jay Rodgers. Jay is a successful entrepreneur who has started, grown, and sold well over a dozen companies, netting millions of dollars in the process. Because he appreciates the impact entrepreneurs can have on this country, he has spent a great deal of his time over the years mentoring them one-on-one. He wanted to have a more powerful impact and a greater influence on more people than he could have with his own limited time. So he stepped back and asked, "What can I devote the rest of my life to that would give ongoing perpetual motion to the fostering and support of successful entrepreneurship?" By leveraging his own circle of friends and business associates, Biz Owners' Ed was born.

Jay initially enlisted the support of his wife Bettye, David Hammer, Jim Attrell, Rick Garrett, and Dave Casey as co-founders. They all shared a concern about the tremendous growth in governmental control of business, which is moving America away from the free enterprise system that has made our country the greatest country in the world. Although Jay has invested the majority of his time the last 15 years helping entrepreneurs, he found he was spending too much time with people who weren't committed or serious enough about building the job creating companies in the private sector that are the backbone of our country's greatness.

The founders recognized an enormous need for support for serious learners, devoted entrepreneurs, and disciplined high achievers by providing opportunities for them to learn from expert advisors who have successfully dealt with the same challenges they are facing. Higher education was not the answer. Although the higher education system and its tenured professors are well qualified to teach science, literature, history, and many other subjects, most of the professors have never agonized over how they were going to make the next payroll or fund the company's progress. And most have probably never mortgaged their home and future to keep their company alive. Therefore, they're neither equipped nor able to provide the gamut of support required for teaching entrepreneurship. Although Jay taught a Starting Your Own Business class at the University of North Texas and was a guest speaker at the Caruth Institute for Entrepreneurship at SMU's Cox School of Business, he felt he could make a bigger impact in a different setting with a different audience.

Designing and developing the program took over a year and a half, and the first class assembled on January 8, 2013. The class is

ENTREPRENEURIAL REFLECTIONS

ONE ENTREPRENEUR'S PERSONAL MOMENTS THAT WILL EXPAND AND CHANGE YOUR THINKING

limited to only twelve members each year so the participants can travel schedule permits. Additionally, as an indication of their sincere desire to help entrepreneurs, they must write a $5,000 check to the Business Owners Ed 501(3)(c) non-profit organization when accepted as a mentor. It is significant that 80% of the individuals invited by Biz to become mentors have accepted the invitation. Many go beyond the ten-week formal program and have established on-going mentor/mentee relationships with its graduates.

One of the mentors in Biz Owners' Ed is Tony Hartl, a successful young entrepreneur who created a company called Planet Tan and subsequently sold it for millions of dollars. Tony was featured in *Inc. Magazine* and *Fortune Small Business*, among others. Because he has a passion for mentoring entrepreneurs, Tony wrote the book *Selling Sunshine* about his own journey.

The Biz Owners' Ed team is very deliberate and cautious about inviting guest speakers, most of whom own businesses that service and support small businesses. Guest speakers are there to provide only immediate and actionable information of value to entrepreneurs, not to solicit in any form or fashion clients for their particular businesses. Any guest speaker uttering a single solicitous line during the presentation is not invited back.

Biz Owners' Ed has been tremendously successful, and the stories of the growth and successes of its class members are numerous and wonderful to celebrate. A member of its first class in January 2013 owned a business that had gross revenue of $10.5 million in 2012. He credits the Biz Owners' Ed program with playing a significant role in moving his company revenues to over $24 million in 2014.

The Biz Owners' Ed program is a great platform for entrepreneurs to get honest feedback from their peers and from entrepreneurs who have already achieved success. This program should be in every major city because it helps entrepreneurs grow their businesses and create more private sector small business jobs. In every session, entrepreneurs are inspired so much by the stories shared and the advice they get that it changes their business.

If you have already climbed your entrepreneurial mountains, maybe you should start a Biz Owners' Ed type program of your own to help mentor other entrepreneurs. Contact us by visiting the website: **www.BizOwnersEd.org**. The founders are willing and anxious to help you launch your program. Because the program's only goal is to help seriously committed entrepreneurs, your program does not even need to mention Biz Owners' support.

ENTREPRENEURIAL
REFLECTIONS

LESSONS AT A GLANCE

1. *Be willing to take risks. If you're an entrepreneur, it's inevitable that you'll eventually be the only one who believes in a decision you've got to make. That means you've got to go against the grain and take risks.*

2. *Entrepreneurs are willing to bet on themselves.*

3. *Entrepreneurs do what it takes to accomplish the goal.*

4. *Be different. When you play to win big, you won't win them all, but you won't get lost in the crowd.*

5. *You do not always need all the facts or eyes on the investment to make the right decisions. In order to win, bet on winners. In most transactions, you are betting primarily on people. Follow your gut.*

6. *Often people standing quietly on the sidelines can provide valuable information.*

7. *Entrepreneurs always find a different way. Don't rush into accepting investor money. Your ideal investors will bring more to the table than just money.*

8. *Look for opportunities to divide and multiply.*

9. *Look at all sides of the transaction.*

10. *No one says "yes" to a question that you do not ask.*

11. *You never learn if or how to deal with someone in business unless you understand what motivates them and how to help them achieve their goals.*

12. *There is a lot to be said for learning from our mistakes.*

13. *You don't need to be the world's greatest hunter to shoot the biggest bear.*

14. *Don't let big overshadow profitable.*

15. *Taking time to contact the debtor and asking if he or she would like me to buy their loan totally changes the relationship and dynamics.*

16. *Sometimes it's easier and more profitable to change the players than to change the game.*

17. *Make sure your business includes having fun.*

18. *Dollars are only a small part of compensation.*

19. *Selling a product or business doesn't have to be about addressing needs.*

20. *Sell to what people want, and you'll always win.*

21. *Build a legacy and a business based on integrity.*

22. *The very best contract is one that clearly and simply expresses all parties' intents, is signed, and then put in a filing cabinet never to be retrieved.*

23. *Draw your own conclusions and plan and negotiate accordingly.*

24. *As you build your business, make sure that you, not a supplier or a customer, are in charge and in control of your*

destiny.

25. *Mistakes are a part of life. Admit them, address them, and move on.*

26. *Do your research and understand what motivates someone.*

27. *Don't predict. Protect.*

28. *Always look for the gems that hide in the rubble.*

29. *Take decisive action.*

30. *It's only business; it's not personal.*

31. *If you maintain your ethics and integrity, you can disagree on business issues without destroying personal relationships.*

32. *Take time to know your stakeholders and look at the business through their eyes.*

33. *Choose your fights carefully. Are they really worth the time, effort, and expense?*

34. *Define your market on the front end, and don't lose money trying to be all things to all people.*

35. *Choose a tagline and logo that is simple and memorable.*

36. *If you're not getting a lot of "no's," you're missing a lot of "yes's."*

37. *Use "No" as the starting point, not as the finish line.*

38. *The time to address your concerns is before you sign on the line. Do your due diligence and look for ways to reduce your risk.*

39. *Don't be afraid to give or get tough advice.*

40. *Seize the moment.*

41. *Don't allow the short-term benefits to be detrimental to your game winning homerun.*

42. *Be careful if you have a one-trick pony. Look for more tricks or another buyer.*

43. *Leverage your loyalty.*

44. *There's always a market for excellence and quality.*

45. *You can't create a market.*

46. *Opportunity lies in identifying and serving unserved and underserved markets.*

47. *Understand the tax laws and understand your rights.*

48. *Evaluate software not based on the bells and whistles; evaluate it based on the bottom line.*

49. *Know when to step aside.*

50. *Your time is valuable.*

51. *Don't be afraid to disrupt an industry's current processes in favor of a better one.*

52. *Entrepreneurs take calculated risks.*

53. *Agreeing to reevaluate your value after you've proven yourself is more important than your opening salary.*

54. *Great things happen when you ask.*

55. *Don't Forget to ask!*

ENTREPRENEURIAL
REFLECTIONS

SPECIAL
ACKNOWLEDGMENT

O ne of the reasons Biz Owners' Ed was created is because the founders understand the power of entrepreneurs working and learning together. You can do much more with the help of others than you can alone. One of the important people in my life is David Hammer, an attorney and now close friend who has been with me through several important deals. *Entrepreneurial Reflections* would never have been published had it not been for David. On a Trans-Atlantic cruise, David sat me down and over several days personally typed the first manuscript as I told the stories. Hopefully by his own story you can see that life and business is a patchwork of deals, changes, and also opportunity. If you feel like you've lost one opportunity or position, it might just be a stepping stone to another one.

David got his law degree three years after he left his CPA career at Deloitte and joined a Dallas law firm where his practice was dedicated almost exclusively to mergers and acquisitions work. After nine years, that firm broke up following the sale of its large publicly-held client on which he had spent almost all of his time. David gained a lot of street smarts and business experience in the aftermath of that firm's breakup. He joined a second law firm based in Fort Worth that only lasted for 11 months but which put him in contact with the general counsel at Radio Shack for whom he worked in effecting the acquisition by Radio Shack of a circuit board manufacturer in Salt Lake City. After the breakup of that second law firm, David received a call from Radio Shack's general counsel asking if he had ever done any international transactions.

After answering "yes" and detailing his international experience, David was asked to represent Radio Shack in its acquisition of a ten-country company based in Stockholm, Sweden. They concluded that transaction for a purchase price of $155 Million in cash, and that transaction began a 10-year period where he was the outside counsel to Radio Shack for its mergers and acquisitions work. That relationship continued until both Radio Shack's general counsel and deputy general counsel retired at about the same time. By then, he was already also representing numerous entrepreneurs and had been invited to serve on a number of corporate boards, many of which I was involved in. One of those board relationships led to an opportunity to serve that client as a sell-side investment banker and advisor. Following the sale of that business to Textron, David chose to continue to represent others in that same capacity, and he still does so today. So from a beginning where he represented large public companies as a CPA and later as an attorney, David now exclusively represents entrepreneurs in legal and investment banking transactions in what is a multi-faceted career spanning 170+ M & A transactions for over $1 Billion in enterprise value. Entrepreneurs appreciate that David doesn't charge based on his time and effort. He charges a success fee that is only paid when the sale funds.

David and I have been through a lot of deals together. He has handled the sale of thirteen entities that I played the major role in.

He's been a great friend and partner. We've had an incredible amount of fun working and playing together. If it weren't for David and Bettye, this book wouldn't be possible. The lesson in all of this is that you can be the greatest entrepreneur in the world, but if you don't have a life team supporting you, you'll only be half as effective.

ENTREPRENEURIAL
REFLECTIONS

ONE ENTREPRENEUR'S

PERSONAL MOMENTS

THAT WILL EXPAND AND

CHANGE YOUR THINKING.

JAY D. RODGERS